GETTING TO KNOW YOU

A guide to record-keeping in early childhood education and care

LYNNE BARTHOLOMEW & TINA BRUCE

Hodder & Stoughton
LONDON SYDNEY AUCKLAND

British Library Cataloguing in Publication Data

Bartholomew, Lynne
  Getting to Know You: Guide to
  Record-keeping in Early Childhood
  I. Title II. Bruce, Tina
  372.19

ISBN 0–340–57632–4

First published 1993

Impression number	10 9 8 7 6 5 4 3 2 1
Year	1998 1997 1996 1995 1994 1993

Typeset by Wearset, Boldon, Tyne and Wear
Printed in Great Britain for the educational publishing division of Hodder & Stoughton Ltd, Mill Road, Dunton Green, Sevenoaks, Kent by Thomson Litho Ltd.

This book is dedicated to our children, Tom, Simon, Hannah and Tom, from whom we have learned so much.

<u>Acknowledgments</u>

Thanks to Joyce Bradley, June Byne, Lorraine Harding and Clare McIsaac, who have worked so hard in contributing to this book.

Thanks also to Margaret Sargent for her unfailing support and for taking many of the photographs; and to the following for allowing us to use their materials: Jennifer Buckle; Peter Thompstone; Debbie Bourne; Sheila Vizard and the Allenby school staff; Margy Whalley; Katey Mairs and the Pen Green staff; Joyce French and the Bridlington staff; Ann Hedley and colleagues; Beryl McDougall and colleagues involved in compiling the Cleveland *Rumpus Schema Extra* book; to Ann Alderman; Meg Knott and colleagues in Barnet; to Janet Yerbury in Merton; Wendy Jory at Hammersmith and Fulham and Patricia Juanette; Karen McCloud and the James Lee Nursery staff; Jean Stevens; Pat Gura and the Froebel Blockplay Research Group; the staff at Greenmead school and the children and their families everywhere.

CONTENTS

Series Preface – 0–8 Years: The First Phase Of Living

At most times in history, and in most parts of the world, the first eight years of life have been seen as the first phase of living. Ideally, during this period, children learn who they are; about those who are significant to them; and how their world is. They learn to take part, and how to contribute creatively, imaginatively, sensitively and reflectively.

Children learn through and with the people they love and the people who care for them. They learn through being physically active, through real, direct experiences, and through learning how to make and use symbolic systems, such as play, language and representation. Whether children are at home, in nursery schools, classes, family centres, day nurseries, or playgroups, workplace nurseries, primary schools or whatever, they need informed adults who can help them. The series will help those who work with young children, in whatever capacity, to be as informed as possible about this first phase of living. From the age of eight years all the developing and learning can be consolidated, hopefully in ways which build on what has gone before.

In this series, different books emphasise different aspects of the first phase of living. *Getting to Know You* and *Learning to be Strong* give high status to adults (parents and early-childhood specialists of all kinds) who love and work with children. *Getting to Know You*, by Lynne Bartholomew and Tina Bruce focuses on the importance of adults in the lives of children. Observing children in spontaneous situations at Redford House Nursery, (a workplace nursery) and in a variety of other settings, the book emulates the spirit of Susan Isaacs. This means using theory to interpret observations and recording the progress of children as they are supported and extended in their development and learning. The book is full of examples of good practice in record-keeping. Unless we know and understand our children, unless we act effectively on what we know, we cannot help them very much.

Learning to be Strong by Margy Whalley, helps us to see how important it is that all the adults living with or working with children act as a team. This is undoubtedly one of the most important kinds of partnership that human beings ever make. When adults come together and use their energy in an orchestrated way on behalf of the child, then quality and excellent progress are seen. Pen Green Family Centre is the story of the development of a kind of partnership which Margaret McMillan would have admired.

Just as the first two books emphasise the importance of the adult helping the child, the next two focus *on* the child. John Matthews helps us to focus on one of the ways in which children learn to use symbolic systems. In *Representation in Childhood*, he looks at how children keep hold of the experiences they have through the process of representation. Children's drawings and paintings are looked at in a way which goes beyond the superficial, and help us to understand details. This means the adult can help the child better. Doing this is a complex process, but the book suggests ways which are easy to understand, and is full of real examples.

Later in the series, Mollie Davies looks at *Movement* (which includes dance) and its major contributions to development and learning. She focuses on actions, as well as representations, play and language, demonstrating that movement is truly one of the basics. She gives many practical examples to help those working with children enjoy movement with confidence, bringing together actions, feelings, thoughts and relationships.

Other books in the series will underline the importance of adults working together to become informed in order to help children develop and learn.

Clinging to dogma, 'I believe children need...' or saying 'What was good enough for me...' is not good enough. Children deserve better than that. The pursuit of excellence means being informed. This series will help adults increase their knowledge and understanding of the 'first phase of living', and to act in the light of this for the good of children.

TINA BRUCE

A thought before you read this book: *There is in fact no other area of study so important to the human race as the study of its children.*

Lesley Webb (1975, p.89)

INTRODUCTION

This is a book about the process of finding user-friendly and purposeful ways of record-keeping. It is designed to help those working with young children and their families in a variety of settings in the first eight years of a child's life. It is about looking with insight at children and providing them with what they need in order to develop and learn optimally. It looks at the history of record-keeping, and describes examples of good practice in both education, care and health settings. It also helps to monitor a child's progress and to work out what is needed next.

All the examples of record-keeping given in this book can be linked with either the National Curriculum (in England and Wales) or the 5–14 Guidelines (in Scotland) to fulfil legal requirements where necessary. However, this cannot be done in a prescriptive way because the authors of this book share the concerns of many parents and educators of all kinds working with young children, that these must be a resource, but never a strait-jacket.

Glossary

This glossary contains some of the important terms used in this book. You might want to refer to this before you read the book, while you read the book, or use the glossary as a way of pulling together some of the strands explored in the book.

Anecdotal Records

These can be written, annotated photographs (often of constructions, dances, action in the sand, water, garden) or examples of paintings, drawings etc. They are compiled on quiet reflection, alone, with a colleague or parent, or with the child, after the event has taken place. (For example at the end of the day, or the end of the week.) Because of this, it may only be possible to give a rough date and time of day when the observation was made.

They are a useful way of adding to and enhancing the other kinds of records, and are often helpful in adding detail to scrapbooks and records of achievement, but they are not as reliable or accurate as other methods if they are made too long after the event, because our memories can sometimes play tricks on us.

Diaries

These are dated anecdotal records, but because they are kept on a daily basis, they can become a great burden.

Evaluative Records

These help us to forward plan, organise, manage and review what we offer to children and their families. They involve us in making long-term plans e.g. FLOW charts and in seeing 'Possible Lines of Direction' that might be taken (PLOD charts) as well as weekly and daily plans which link with the formative records we keep of the individual child's progress.

FORMATIVE RECORDS

These are records which build up gradually and continuously over time. They are the most useful kind of record, as they help us to see how individual children are learning, and how we are helping them to learn well. They will involve us in keeping narrative records. Formative records emphasise the process of developing and learning and help us to monitor progress.

NARRATIVE RECORDS

There are several different kinds of narrative record, but they all aim to give the date, time of day when the observation was made, and duration of the observation, albeit with varying degrees of preciseness. Anecdotes are the least precise, compared with running records or specimen records which are both made on-the-spot. Narrative records use the following methods: writing, diagrams, sketches, audio and video tape recordings and photographs.

ON-THE-SPOT RECORDS

1 Running records

These are made on-the-spot, and note what the child does and says (i.e. actions and language). The date, starting and finishing time is noted. Later on, the observation can be added to (using a different coloured pen, since these will be anecdotal records). Later that day (ideal) or if not, at the end of the week, running records can also be looked at with a particular focus, or can be coded in particular ways.

2 Specimen records

These are also made on-the-spot. They note actions and language, as well as information about the situation and place. Again, the date, starting and finishing time is noted. Details can be filled out later (with a different colour pen, as the additions are anecdotal records).

Because specimen records give actions, language and context in which these took place, they are able to yield rich quantities of information, which can be reflected on later that day (ideal) or later that week to take a particular focus, or to code according to particular emphases.

SCHEMAS

Schemas are a set of repeatable actions, which can be generalised in different situations. The experiences of life are integrated into these patterns and are gradually co-ordinated. Co-ordinations lead to higher-level and more powerful schemas. (Athey 1990, pp.35–7).

SUMMATIVE RECORDS

At regular intervals, we shall need to take stock of where a child is in development and learning and of what we are offering the child and the family. Summative records help us to review what is going on at a particular time.

The most useful summative records can be compiled easily from the formative records, by giving them a particular FOCUS, by looking at the way they have been CODED, by reviewing the FLOW or PLOD charts, and related EVALUATION records. These can be used when sharing progress with parents, colleagues in the same setting, or colleagues from other agencies.

Standardised tests of various kinds are useful in confirming (or not) progress, and help to pin-point (diagnose) strengths and difficulties. If standardised summative tests dominate, they lose their usefulness, and children become tested, instead of the emphasis being on helping children to develop and learn. Summative records focus on results and products, rather than how these came about.

GETTING TO KNOW THIS BOOK

In Chapter 1, the impact of the DES Report *Starting with Quality* (1990), the National Curriculum, and the Children Act (1989) is considered as a backcloth to the way we approach record-keeping from babyhood to the eighth year of life. In Chapter 2, we maintain a steady course in early childhood education by building on good practice in record-keeping, using the past as a resource. Chapter 3 considers current good practice in the same spirit. Chapter 4 looks at record-keeping and its continuing development at Redford House Nursery, Roehampton Institute (RI). In this way, we share the process that staff at Redford House Nursery have experienced, getting to know the influences on them, the influences from the past, what others are doing about record-keeping who share the same early childhood principles, and getting to know what they want to do in developing purposeful, user-friendly record-keeping.

GETTING TO KNOW ABOUT REDFORD HOUSE NURSERY

Redford House Nursery opened in November 1989 to serve the staff and students of Richmond, Twickenham and Roehampton Health Authority (RTRHA) and of Roehampton Institute (RI). The Nursery is managed by the Health Authority.

It is a workplace nursery licensed to take thirty-five children at any one time, with an adult child ratio of 1:8. Children attending are aged between two-and-a-half and five years inclusive. Some children attend daily, others are part-time. The nursery opens from 7.15 am to 6.00 pm throughout the year. Staff work across three shifts, 7.15 am to 3.30 pm, 8.30 am to 5.10 pm or 9.30 am to 6.00 pm. There is a holiday play scheme for children up to seven years to fill places while students are on summer vacation.

The co-ordinator is a Senior Lecturer in early childhood education based at Froebel Institute College, RI, teaching on the BA (QTS) and in-service courses during term-time. She is based four days a week in Redford House Nursery in term-time and five days otherwise. Staff are all NNEB qualified.

Because of the long hours that the nursery remains open, and the lack of closures during school holidays, there are many practical constraints which cut across the time and energy available to think about and develop good record-keeping. The shift system of working means that staff meetings have to be at 6.00 pm which is exhausting for staff who have worked the first shift and have to return. After a whole day's work which is physically, emotionally and intellectually demanding, not to mention the impact of dealing with a whole range of relationships with children, parents and colleagues, it is unlikely that staff will be at their most alert and creative. Tricia David (1992) indicates that staff at Redford House are not alone. Nevertheless, the staff remain determined to do their own thinking and gain control and a sense of ownership over the way they tackle the challenges presented when developing a useful, purposeful and user-friendly approach to record-keeping.

As it is a workplace nursery, it is difficult for parents to be available, apart from pre-visits, to spend time in the nursery. Some parents travel from as far as 50 miles away, so that home-visiting is not possible. The staff firmly believe, however, that working with parents is an integral part of providing appropriately across the curriculum for every child. In order to achieve this, staff members each have a family group and liaise particularly with the parents in their group. Parent evenings are arranged when parents can come and discuss their child, but this is not always practicable for parents living a long distance away. Parent evenings, when a speaker is arranged (for example to talk about early literacy), have the same practical considerations.

Traditionally valued provision is always available according to the principles of the self-servicing or workshop environment. The outside area is considered as important as the inside.

This introduction to Redford House Nursery serves as a backcloth to Chapter 4, which looks at the way staff developed their record-keeping.

1 GETTING TO KNOW THE CHILD

WHY KEEP RECORDS?

We need to keep records so that staff and parents can do their best for each child. Through getting to know the child, we get to know how to help that child develop in all aspects and learn more. We get to know what to offer the child next. Getting to know the child is about:

- The child's progress = **assessment**

- What we have offered, are offering
  and will offer the child next = **evaluation**
- Our records will need to **link** assessment with evaluation

There is no 'royal road' to record-keeping. Each team in each setting will need to find its own way, including parents and children as part of the process. The record-keeping used will need to feel owned by everybody working with it.

Observing spontaneous play helps us to plan

THE INFLUENCES UPON US

It is almost impossible not to be influenced by the historic and cultural era in which we operate. At the moment, those working with young children are, whether conscious of it or not, inextricably linked with what is happening in relation to current official policy in Britain. The atmosphere produced by three documents which focus on young children is very pervasive. These are:

1   The *Starting with Quality* Report (DES, 1990)
2   The Children Act 1989
3   The National Curriculum

Getting to Know You started out because a group of people working together decided it was important to focus on record-keeping as part of the development plans for their work with children and families.

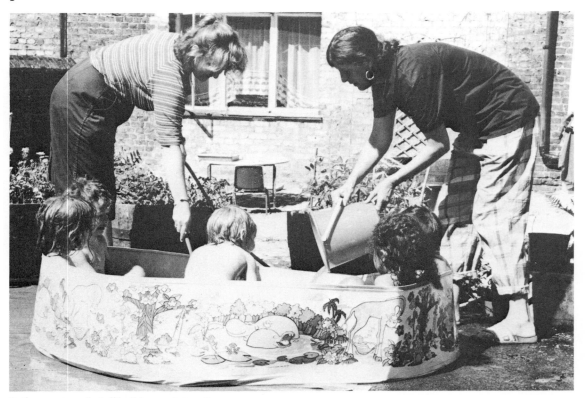

Both parents and staff build records together

The three documents mentioned have influenced this process both consciously and probably unconsciously. When the present influences us at an unconscious level, its impact is usually powerful, as is propaganda or subliminal advertising. It is therefore important to become conscious of the influences upon us.

'Starting with quality' (DES, 1990)

This stresses that record-keeping, observing, assessing, evaluation and reporting are essential, and that every institution should develop a system for it (p.17, paragraph 129–32). *We suggest the aim might be to record:*

(a) *information and insight shared and produced by staff and parents and by children themselves;*
(b) *progress in a child's development as an effective learner in a group setting, including social and emotional development;*
(c) *progress in attainment in skills and concepts for which the curriculum provides;*
(d) *group curriculum provision; its planning, implementation and evaluation.*

The Report also recommends that 'research should be commissioned in order to develop such guidance to help both to inform and to improve what is offered to the under-fives and post-five provision.'

A good quality curriculum for young children is not possible without good record-keeping and reporting. Although *Starting with Quality* stresses this, it can only plead for more research to guide practitioners. It is easy to agree that quality record-keeping is 'a good thing', but it is quite another to develop good systems for doing this when no additional resources are to be made available.

Of course, no one would want to be told what to do in relation to record-keeping. However it does seem from conversations with colleagues working with young children in different parts of the country, and in a variety of settings, that people would certainly appreciate help, support, and concrete encouragement in developing their own strategies for tackling such a demanding, challenging and difficult area.

The *Starting with Quality* Report (p.17, paragraph 130) summarises the situation for under-fives but can also be applied to older children who are required to follow the National Curriculum.

> *What is done to record and report children's progress will, nevertheless, be subject to a large extent to the constraints of time and the circumstances under which education for the under-fives is provided.*

The Children Act (1989)

The spirit behind the Act is already producing positive changes leading to more training becoming available for those in the voluntary sector, social services and health including child minders, welfare assistants, playgroup leaders, health visitors, nursery nurses and parents. This will have a constructive influence on record-keeping, although as Peter Moss's article (1992) points out, there still exists a gulf between education and care services for the child. Anyone trying to keep good records spanning both education and care of the child is going to find it a great challenge within the limits of present resources and training. The more teachers, nursery nurses, playgroup leaders, health visitors, child minders and parents work together, the better the progress that will be made.

We need adequate staff/child ratios

If we are to make good records, we need space during the day to write them. Tricia David (1990 p.98) stresses this. The Children Act 1989 recommends a staff ratio of 8:1 for children from three to five years in day nurseries. The Pre-school Playgroup Association recommends 5:1 for a playgroup. Nursery schools have a 13:1 ratio, nursery classes 15:1 in England and Wales, whilst in reception classes, many four-year-olds experience 30:1 and sometimes more. One of the most practical ways of dealing with unsatisfactory adult/child ratios is to target one child a day (or more if possible) so that in-depth observations are made approximately every three to four weeks. We need the courage to remember that one in-depth observation is worth thirty superficial daily ones. The Hammersmith and Fulham LEA nursery records points out that 'Because young children develop in an integrated way, the same observation may yield information about several aspects of the child's progress.'

The National Curriculum

By law, four-year-olds in reception classes at primary schools (eighty per cent according to Pascal, 1990) must follow the National Curriculum if the majority of the children in the classes are five years old. This contrasts with four-year-olds in nursery classes, schools, playgroups, at home, with child minders, in family centres, combined centres, private schools or daycare, or workplace nurseries. These children do not experience so sharply the downward pressure of the National Curriculum. In this book, care has been taken not to over emphasise the minimum educational requirements of the National Curriculum, but to keep it in balance with the broader educational and general needs of the youngest children emphasised in the *Starting with Quality* Report and the needs of all children under eight years old which are given focus in the Children Act.

REDFORD HOUSE NURSERY AND RECORD-KEEPING

Against this backcloth, the staff made record-keeping the priority in their development plans, arising from a real need to find something manageable that worked for them. Not long after its opening, the staff managed to begin a review of their record-keeping, beginning with the question 'Why keep records?' and decided records are important in order to get to know the child in every aspect, and provide what the child needs. A review of the historic background to present-day approaches in record-keeping, and a look at current work, has helped them to value their early-childhood philosophy, and to build on its strengths in developing good records. Staff feel strong in their understanding of individual children and their needs, helped by the family worker approach described in the introduction.

Getting to know the child

The nursery nurses are trained in child observation and are particularly strong in being able to use minute observation techniques for diagnostic purposes such as running records, specimen records or anecdotal records (see Chapter 2). This helps them to create a picture, a vignette of the whole child. They are also able, through in-service training, to observe generalised patterns in an individual child's development, and can adjust what they offer the child to further that child's learning. By providing for individual children, they can also use records to cater for groups of children. This is discussed later in the book.

The review showed that all staff value the need for good observation of individual children, and are concerned to use this to inform their curriculum organisation and planning. They want to support children using traditionally successful early-years provision of materials, opportunities, experiences and relationships with others. They also want to improve their effectiveness in extending children in their learning, working as a team whilst acting as individual family workers. They see good record-keeping as central to this process. This book shows how specimen records traditionally used by early childhood workers remain the basis of record-keeping, but are gradually put to better use, becoming less time and energy consuming, and more effective. This is because one observation gives a clue, and the build up of continuous observations can be used to reflect on the child's progress from various view-points, for example relationships, developments in play, mathematics, language and literacy or imagination.

Record-keeping is part of the continual learning process of the staff at Redford House, as it is with all of us working with young children and their families. Record-keeping is about getting to know the child to the best of our ability, in ways which do not cause us to burn out or to give up, despite the enormity of the challenge with present constraints upon us. Without good record-keeping, we cannot work well.

2 GETTING TO KNOW WHERE WE ARE COMING FROM

POWERFUL LESSONS FROM THE PAST

If we look back to the lessons that history can teach us, they are powerful ones. The current debates in the 1990s about record-keeping are not new ones. They have raged in one form or another at least since the middle of the eighteenth century. They have never been resolved, and we cannot expect to resolve them completely today. However, we can try to see with clarity what the main issues have always been, and how people have tackled them. We can identify the principles which occur again and again in the keeping of good records. Having identified them, we can translate them in terms of the setting we work in today, and so make good records, feel ownership of them, and confidence in them. Record-keeping is an integral part of our whole approach to working with young children and those close to them. It cannot be split off from everything else that we do. Almy (1975) p.227 stated

> ...unless it helps teachers to capitalise on children's strength and support their weaknesses, such procedures had better be abandoned ... Records have value only to the extent that the staff puts them to use in guiding and instructing children.

There is probably considerable agreement that keeping records is 'a good thing' but as the song says, 'It ain't what you do, it's the way that you do it'. That is what this chapter is about.

BABY BIOGRAPHIES IN THE EIGHTEENTH CENTURY

We know that it is the people who love children and who are committed to them who are prepared to go to great lengths for them. It is not therefore surprising that the first examples of quality record-keeping were made by parents. Until the end of the eighteenth century the infant mortality rate was high in the first year of life, but in 1774, Johann Heinrich Pestalozzi wrote *A Father's Diary* about his three-and-a-half-year-old son. In 1787 Dietrich

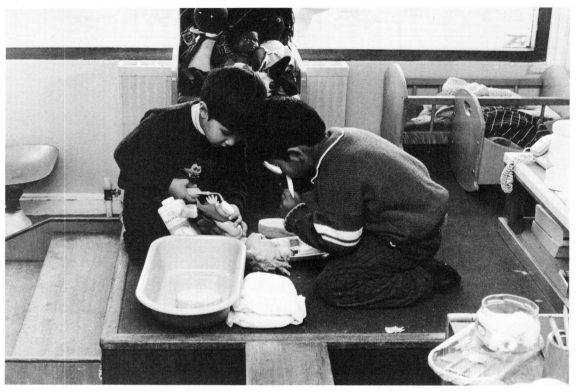

Observing play in natural settings helps narrative records to be kept

Tiedmann wrote about his son's first three years of life. In 1877 Charles Darwin published the observations of his son Doddy, (William Erasmus) based on observations made thirty-seven years before. (See Irwin and Bushnell, 1980; Navarra, 1955.)

What we can learn from the eighteenth-century baby biographies

1   Early baby biographies demonstrate how important it is to look, listen and enjoy being with children. It is only through doing this that we can really get to know a child and understand the child's development and learning.
2   Baby biographies remind us of the importance of being in a natural setting. Irwin & Bushnell (1980 p.5) point out that '. . . each child exhibits his or her own preferred learning style if the adult will just watch for clues.'
3   Our own personal philosophy of life influences what we observe. The observations we make and the records we keep are direct products of our framework of thinking, feeling and relating to children and their families. Sylva & Moore (1984) found that records kept in tightly structured nurseries

tended to use check-lists, while indirectly and informally structured nurseries kept narrative-type records. In other words, the philosophy of the staff affects the record-keeping style.

4   Knowing what our philosophy is empowers our work. If we are not aware of the philosophy that influences us, our observations will be random, uninformed and so incapable of being used to inform our forward-planning and organisation of the curriculum. Irwin & Bushnell say (1980 p.3)

> once we have trained ourselves to become keen observers, we can turn our attention to becoming shrewd interpreters of what we observe. What we see, and what we think about what we see, will naturally raise questions as to what actions we might take. Identifying, recording, hypothesising, questioning, theorising, changing, these are all part of the cycle of discovery for every observer.

Charles Darwin moved through this whole cycle, and his records, including his baby biography of Doddy, contributed to the revolution in thinking about the origin and development of the species.

5   We cannot separate observation from recording. We cannot record unless we observe. In order to keep good records, baby biographies from the eighteenth century teach us that we need to observe so that we can support and extend the development and learning of the child (Bruce, 1987; 1991).

6   Parents are central to this process.

THE CHILD STUDY MOVEMENT

Irwin & Bushnell (1980 p.23) suggest that three men contributed to the emergence of the child study movement during the period spanning the 1870s to the 1950s. Charles Darwin (1809–82) who, as we have seen published his observations of his son, Doddy in 1877. Granville Stanley Hall (1846–1924) founded the *American Journal of Psychology* and organised conferences hosted at Clark University. His students included Dewey, Gessell and Terman. Irwin & Bushnell (p.25) suggest that Darwin's influence and Hall's enthusiasm and promotion led to the burgeoning of the Child Study Movement. It was further promoted when Lawrence Kelso Frank (1890–1968) administered the grants of the Spelman Rockefeller Memorial in the 1920s which brought wide disseminaton.

The home-based baby biographies written by parents such as Charles Darwin, gave way to child studies written by professionals trained in observation, and eager to analyse. Some of the professionals (such as Navarra, 1955) studied their own children.

Child studies have not been so widespread since the 1960s but as we shall see in the next sections, publications making use of them are greatly valued because they give us such insight as children develop and learn. More than anything else, they show us how to provide children with what they need.

What we can learn from the Child Study Movement

1   **When parents and professional workers join together, they make a powerful and constructive partnership.** Parents have always been deeply involved in the development and learning of their children. They were amongst the first record keepers of their children's progress. The Froebel Nursery Project (1972–77) directed by Chris Athey, demonstrated that parents are hungry for help in this area, and deeply appreciative of it. More recently, Martin Hughes (1990, 1991) echoes the fact that parents want to work closely with professionals. They are not out to challenge. They want to become informed together with the educators who work with their child and to share their child's progress with them in a spirit of partnership. During this century, parents have continued to make child studies. For example, Piaget in the 1920s, Navarra in 1955, Bissex, Grübacker and Matthews in the 1980s.

Piaget 1920s
His early work involved observing his three children in natural settings. This is probably when he did his best work. Unfortunately he later switched to comparing test groups of children on adult-set tasks in laboratory settings. This led to a serious under-estimation of what children can achieve, since tests do not allow children to function at their highest levels (Donaldson, 1978).

Navarra 1955
John Navarra and his wife observed and recorded the development of scientific concepts in their six-year-old son L.B. in the home situation. Two important points are made by Navarra (p.26) 'all data no matter what the source, must be viewed in context against a complete pattern.' However, one example may serve as a clue or pointer. Secondly, he is clear that spontaneous activity yields the most useful information for record-keeping (p.20) 'The study of play activity becomes the most important device by which insight was gained concerning the conceptual development of the child.' Navarra adds (p.30) 'on the few occasions when he [L.B.] was put on the spot, superficial replies were obtained.'

Everyday life provides a natural setting for observations

Ruth Weir 1970s

Ruth Weir's study of her two-year-old son Anthony and his pre-sleep monologues have proved invaluable for those researching language development, as have other studies such as Paul West's *Words for a Deaf Daughter*, or Glenda Bissex looking at her son Paul's early writing and reading from five-and-a-half-years to eleven-years.

John Matthews 1988

John Matthews has made a longitudinal study of the drawings, paintings and constructions of his three children, Ben, Joel and Hannah from birth to adolescence. These are mainly in the home setting, since he was present while they were drawing, painting and constructing. His work will be explored in depth in his book to be published later in this series.

2   **Being clear about our philosophy means that we can look at other theories critically and with interest.** It is not the intention of this book to spend time examining in great detail the influence of behaviourist psychology theory on record-keeping from the 1920s. Suffice it to say that overall it has had the

damaging impact of over-valuing unnatural settings, adult-led pre-structured tasks and introducing pre-structured record sheets. Records of children were confined to those who could or could not manage to do what the adult's task required, and a 'sheep and goats' element began to creep in. Christine Hardyman writes (1984 p.165) 'Frederick Truby King and John B. Watson both came to the study of children from the study of animals, and their debts to it are all too obvious'.

Chris Athey sums up this approach (1990 p.30)

> *in programmes where the focus is on one way transmission of information, teachers find it difficult to advance their knowledge of child development because so much time is taken up with the content to be transmitted.*

This contrasts with the view taken in this book that sees development as the motor for learning. It emphasises the child as an active learner rather than a passive receiver of knowledge.

3   **We need to tease out the relationship between development and learning.** If we do not do this, we shall not know how we want to work with children and their families, what our records are for, or how to make use of them. We want our records to have purpose and function, to help us provide in educationally worthwhile ways across the curriculum. Otherwise our records will not be worth all the efforts of writing, photographing etc. Joan Tamburrini (1983) suggests that development is about children acting spontaneously. It is about the general situation in which children function. For example, Matthew, at two years old, can run and jump, but he can't yet hop or skip. He loves to run across open spaces, and to jump to music. Learning, she suggests, is not spontaneous. It is sparked by another person or by a situation. Learning is provoked, and limited to the particular situation, moment or specific problem to be tackled: Matthew is taken to a gymnasium and invited to run. He is taken to a country field, where running is more of a problem on a less even surface. He is learning to run in a particular situation. He goes to the fair, where he learns how to jump on an inflatable castle, a specific situation with particular problems.

Most of the learning children do happens as they develop. We don't even notice that they are learning. It is one of nature's safety mechanisms. It is actually difficult to stop children learning providing they are with people who encourage their general development, that is, providing it is known that two-year-olds love to run and jump because developmentally that is what two-year-olds need to do. Children would be constrained from

Learning is sparked off by another person or situation

learning if they were not allowed to develop normally in this way, and we have seen tragic instances of this in the orphanages of Romania where children, sitting in a cot all day, have become mentally retarded partly through their development being constrained. Where general development is constrained through a disability, we also have to be imaginative in providing learning experiences. For example, blind children rarely crawl because it is frightening to set off into the unknown (Chapman, 1978; Nielsson, 1985; Royal National Institute for the Blind, 1993).

The more adults know about general development, the more appropriately they will be able to plan and so extend the child's learning. Records need to show what the adult observes, and how the adult supports and extends using the relationship between development and learning to do so.

4   **We need to look at the implications of being a trained observer and recorder of children's development and learning.** Although baby biographies in the eighteenth century meant those close to the child could savour and share the records later, this did not help adults to plan and

organise the next step in learning. It accentuated past achievements, milestones and growing points. Modern day parents often keep baby albums full of labelled photographs which are treasured for precisely these reasons.

By contrast the Child Study Movement emphasised the use, purpose and function of observation and recording. Adults were not only to observe and support the child's development, they were also to extend by helping the child to learn.

5   **We need to consider how much we should pre-structure what we shall observe** – if we don't how will we know what to record? Sinn, quoted by Navarra, who made a child study in 1894, wrote of the importance of observing and recording what a child does in a natural setting, since what the child does is

> *meaningless and trivial until it is illuminated by some other action days or weeks after; bits of the mosaic from far apart have to be fitted together before it is intelligible.*

In the 1930s, Susan Isaacs also stressed that it is the child's spontaneous interests, feeling and intellectual life which are significant and worthy of recording. When we begin to pre-structure and manipulate the situation, asking children to perform certain tasks so that we can observe and record them on a prepared form, we shall miss most of the vital information we need in order to help them to learn. Bennett & Kell (1989 p.29) state that there is a

> *tendency amongst teachers to limit their assessment to the products of children's work. Rarely did they attempt to ascertain the processes or strategies employed by children in coming to their finished product.*

In Sweden, the words *teaching* and *learning* are the same. In this book we are not using the word *teach* which implies adults transmitting, imposing, invading and dominating the child's life. We prefer to say *helping the child to learn*. This means the adult is a facilitator, catalyst and enabler, who knows when and how to support general development but also knows the crucial moment when children must have the direct help or planned help if they are to learn something specific. Navarra (1955) puts it very well, writing about the child study he and his wife made about their son L.B.'s development in scientific concepts.

*There was no attempt to 'lead the child by the nose.' It should be clear also
that the child was not being 'used'. He was in the best sense of the word aided
and given opportunities with the full knowledge that adults are vitally
interested in him. In the process, a record was made.*

6   **Narrative records seem to be the most useful for early childhood
     educators.** Lesley Webb (1975) emphasises the dangers of deciding in
     advance precisely what ought to be recorded; as she says, children often do
     not behave or function as they ought. What we would like children to know
     is often different from what they really know. In fact they often know more
     than we think. Dorothy Butler's study, *Cushla and Her Books* took place both
     at home and in school. So did that of Gordon Wells in the 1980s. This study
     cast light on why Rosie, aged five, appeared to function poorly at school,
     and how the school could work to create a more enabling environment for
     her. Like Dorothy Butler's study of Cushla, who is a child with special
     needs, Gordon Wells focused on what Rosie did and said rather than on
     what she could not manage to do. Similarly Virginia Axeline's study, *Dibs –
     In Search of Self* (1964) showed what an autistic child could do rather than
     could not do. Narrative records keep emphasising strengths, whilst pre-
     structured record forms can quickly lead to a focus on weakness, failure and
     'can't do.'

7   **If you want to get ahead get a theory.** John and Elisabeth Robertson made a
     series of films in the 1950s using observations they made of children
     separated from their parents. After watching the film about a child called
     John and his separation from his mother, few audiences did not weep a tear.
     The Robertsons were influenced by John Bowlby's theory of separation and
     loss which has since been modified and developed.
         Our observations and records, whether we like it or not, will be using
     our own pet theories. It is best if we know what they are! This was true in
     the Froebel Block Play Research Project directed by Tina Bruce from 1987 to
     1990, (Gura ed. 1992). This project was influenced partly by the work of
     Chris Athey and the inter-actionist theories of Piaget, Vygotsky and Bruner,
     (discussed in Bruce, 1987). It is possible to look at Harriet Johnson's classic
     study of children's block play at Bank Street College in the 1930s and to
     interpret her records in the light of Piagetian schemas and see patterns in what
     the children do. Similarly the records made by Susan Isaacs in the 1930s at the
     Malting House School can also be interpreted in this way.
         All these records have something in common. They are narrative records,
     using words, diagrams, tape recordings and photography to gather on-the-

spot information which can later be used, reflected on and focused in different ways. This kind of record gives a wealth of information which helps us look backwards, be in the present and to move forwards for the child. These records have purpose and function. They are useful to us in a variety of ways.

8   **We need to be scientific rather than pseudo-scientific when we keep records.** In a BBC Horizon interview (1981) Richard Feynman, the Nobel Prize Winning Physicist was clear that it is premature to try and impose on education the kind of measurement and recording techniques used in advanced physics. This is because, as he said, it is much more difficult to accumulate and analyse real and useful information about children developing and learning than it is to study the atom (Bruce 1991, Chapter 7).

In the next section we shall focus on narrative records, because these are the most helpful to early childhood educators.

NARRATIVE RECORDS

Irwin & Bushnell (1980) list these types of narrative record: diaries, anecdotes, running records and specimen records.

1   **Diaries** are kept daily and can be a burden especially with large numbers of children.
2   **Anecdotes** are more user-friendly, even though they lack the same continuity as a diary. The advantages of recording dated anecdotes is that they can be discussed after the children go home and can be a source of deep pleasure as the record-keeper recognises what important experiences children may have had through, for example, sand play. This kind of quiet reflection also helps us to ponder some of the difficulties a particular child may be having. It is not intrusive on the children, who are often not at ease when they see adults observing them with notepads.
3   **Running records** happen on-the-spot, noting a particular continuous behaviour sequence of the child. Stick-on labels on a pad are often favoured, which ensure conciseness and can be noted without the child feeling watched. This gives just enough dated information, so that later on it can be filled out on the child's profile and any photographs taken at the time can be dated and added. Aspects of particular interest can also be coded using a letter code, or different-coloured highlight pens. This sort of

record reaps a wealth of useful information (Goodman, 1973; Clay, 1985; Primary Language Record, 1989).

4   **Specimen records** also note on-the-spot what the child says and does, but they additionally record the situation or context. This gives us enough detail at the time, but again allows us to fill out more later. We can then look at the child's progress as well as what we are offering the child. We can assess, evaluate and link the two. We can plan ahead. Lesley Webb (1975) was an advocate of this kind of narrative record. It is widely used by NNEB nursery nurses, and health visitors (see Chapter 3). (In this book, we use the more digestible term 'on-the-spot record' rather than 'specimen record'.)

Here is an example of a specimen record taken from Lesley Webb's *Making a Start on Child Study*.

	Date of observation Child's name + date of birth		
	+ actual age		
	Short description of situation in which observation		
	is being made.		
Time	What is happening here		Vocalization
here			here

Specimen record from Making a Start on Child Study (1975), *Basil Blackwell, Oxford*

> *Recording of on-going behaviour has to be done at break-neck speed, and even then no one of us, however proficient, can record everything a child does and says as it is happening.*
>
> (Webb, p.46)

We need to develop our own personal codes. Lesley Webb, for example, uses:

Q clenched fist	L⌐ pincer grip
𝅘 spread fingers	→ R moves to the right

She calls this a 'rapid writing code'. This raw data can then be analysed later.

It is well worth the effort and pays off, especially if particular children are targeted on particular days. In this way a child can be observed in detail regularly. One specimen description can give more information about a child's development and learning than any amount of superficial sampling. Every member of staff needs to take part so that knowledge and ideas can be shared. Use highlight pens of different colours, or letter/number codes.

SAMPLING AND RATING TECHNIQUES

Irwin & Bushnell (1980) give three sampling strategies, none of which is very useful to us.

1   **Time sampling** means looking, say every hour, to check what is happening either with a certain child, or with an area such as the home corner, and recording on a prepared pre-structured form using a code. It quickly encourages a superficial approach, and often turns into an elaborate way of demonstrating that no one is using the home corner, or that a child is always playing outside.

2   **Event sampling**, like time sampling, uses a prepared pre-structured form. Helen Dawes (1934) looked at quarrels as they occurred. However, because the prepared form dictates what is recorded, event sampling usually leaves out much of the interesting information that could be obtained.

3   **Check-lists** are of little value. Unlike specimen records which reflect after the observation has been made through a specific focus, check-lists tend to create a narrow focus so that we are inclined only to look out for what is on the prepared list. Everything else is usually ignored. Using Attainment Targets from the National Curriculum as check-lists could be a way towards creating a very narrow approach to the curriculum, and the kind of pre-structured, adult dominated environment that constrains learning. Ann Alderman until recently General Primary Inspector (Early Years Education) writes in the Barnet Record (1990, p.1) 'Tick-lists of any kind are dangerous and have no place …' Perhaps we could even say check-lists have no place as a record-keeping strategy for any adult who wants to focus on a quality curriculum: they give no detail and tell us nothing of the

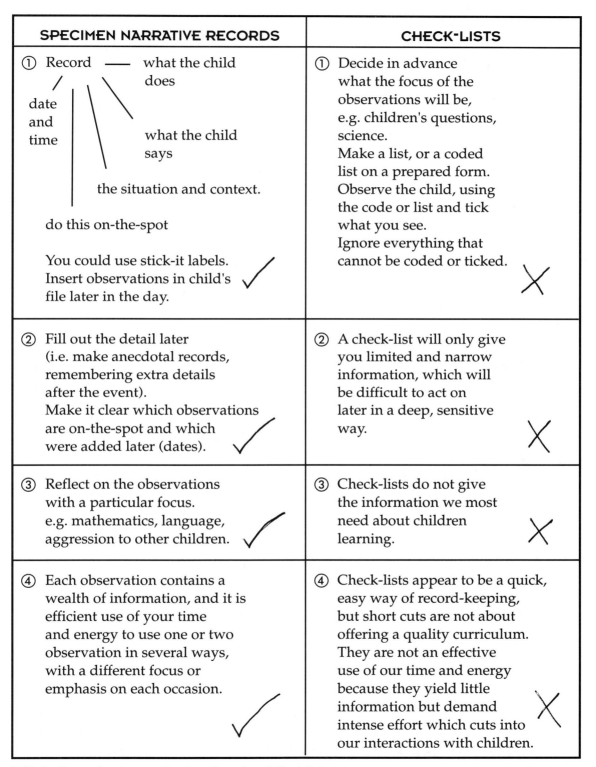

SPECIMEN NARRATIVE RECORDS	CHECK-LISTS
① Record —— what the child does date and time what the child says the situation and context. do this on-the-spot You could use stick-it labels. Insert observations in child's file later in the day. ✓	① Decide in advance what the focus of the observations will be, e.g. children's questions, science. Make a list, or a coded list on a prepared form. Observe the child, using the code or list and tick what you see. Ignore everything that cannot be coded or ticked. ✗
② Fill out the detail later (i.e. make anecdotal records, remembering extra details after the event). Make it clear which observations are on-the-spot and which were added later (dates). ✓	② A check-list will only give you limited and narrow information, which will be difficult to act on later in a deep, sensitive way. ✗
③ Reflect on the observations with a particular focus. e.g. mathematics, language, aggression to other children. ✓	③ Check-lists do not give the information we most need about children learning. ✗
④ Each observation contains a wealth of information, and it is efficient use of your time and energy to use one or two observation in several ways, with a different focus or emphasis on each occasion. ✓	④ Check-lists appear to be a quick, easy way of record-keeping, but short cuts are not about offering a quality curriculum. They are not an effective use of our time and energy because they yield little information but demand intense effort which cuts into our interactions with children. ✗

Table 2   Comparison between Specimen Records and Check-lists

context, or how children learn. Check-lists are unlike specimen records in a very important way. When we use a check-list, we decide in advance what to focus on. When we use a specimen record we do not. We decide afterwards how to focus. We could look at the same observation with a mathematical focus, or to see how easily the child is relating to other children, or to look at the child's play. Check-lists narrow and constrain our focus, and miss out more information than they include. Specimen records help us to be flexible and active in ways which bring deep learning for the child, family and ourselves. (See the Specimen Narrative Records chart on page 19.)

Rating Scales

These can be linked with the introduction of SATS (Standard Assessment Tasks) in Great Britain in 1991, where children as young as six years of age are rated (forty-two per cent of children for SATS for seven-year-olds are in fact six years of age) by being directly observed as they work on pre-structured tasks. They are rated as either working towards or at levels 1, 2, or 3, or as being exceptionally beyond them. This again tells us nothing of causes or context and is time-consuming. It gives little information which we can use for forward planning. Millie Almy (1975) says 'Tests given in the early childhood years are not very good predictors of the child's later status.' The Bullock Report (DES, 1974) reminds us that you do not make children grow by measuring them.

Records need to both assess the child and evaluate the curriculum we offer in ways which link

We have seen that the first records were made by parents. They focused on the child rather than on what the child was offered or would benefit from. In modern life, we still need records which assess the child's progress but we also need records which help us to evaluate the curriculum we provide. It is always best to build on our strengths. Early attempts at evaluating the curriculum tended to make use of prepared charts which adults filled in to see which areas of provision children spontaneously used most frequently, regularly or rarely. This was in the spirit of the bedrock principles of the early childhood traditions, (Bruce, 1987) and, did not attempt to cut across the child's autonomy in learning. It is the intention of this book to keep a steady course of continuity with progression within these traditions.

The emphasis on evaluation in the 1980s that has come about through the introduction of the National Curriculum, has challenged these traditions. Early childhood workers have found ways of recording their evaluations of the curriculum offered as we shall see in the next chapter, keeping faith with their traditional heritage while fulfilling legal requirements. Through re-exploring early childhood work and what it stands for, through re-stating what is important in modern terms, we reaffirm our work and move forward. We can call this process the three R's of early childhood education (Bruce 1988; 1991).

Record-keeping needs to link assessment and evaluation

Linking our records assessing the child's progress, with records evaluating what we offer children, is the challenge for record-keeping as we approach the twenty-first century. Student teachers and nursery nurses on placements have always faced this challenge in the keeping of their placement files. Keeping useful records is probably the most difficult part of working with children, and yet unless we do, we cannot do our best for the children and their families. As we saw in Chapter 1, having established why we want to keep records at all, we need to find ways of doing so which do not wear us out. Burn out is a real issue.

We need a better cross-linking and getting-together of records about individual children with the notes we keep on organisation, planning and provision. What we offer needs to impinge on and relate to how the children react, initiate, or do not. For Tim, aged seven, in a class doing a project on the Romans, the project had no impact. It passed him by. He stolidly continued his interest, which was then the properties of clay, and how birds fly and eat. He was supposed to make 'Roman' pots at school, but he made meticulous clay models of a blackbird, robin, blue tit and woodpecker. The only link with the Romans was the clay. Just as the Romans passed Tim by, so Tim's strengths passed his teacher by. She saw him as a reluctant and poor reader and writer, with a dislike of drawing and an inability to stay on task. By keeping to a pre-structured project (doing the Romans) she was kept from appreciating his deep knowledge of nature, or his advanced ability to make meticulous and exquisite three-dimensional models. She needed a record-keeping system which linked her plans and the Roman project to her individual notes on Tim. In the next chapter we shall look at approaches to record-keeping which make this link.

SUMMARY

- Early records stress assessment. Early Parent/Baby Biographies, and the Child Study Movement encouraged professionals to write their observations of children's progress.

- We need parent/professional partnership in observation of children's progress in order to keep useful records.

- Narrative records are the most informative and efficient use of our time and energy.

- We need to keep records which assess the child and evaluate what we offer the child in ways which link with each other.

- Our records need to build on the bedrock principles which stem from the early-childhood traditions (Bruce, 1987):

1   Childhood is seen as valid in itself, as part of life and not simply as preparation for adulthood. Thus education is seen similarly as something of the present and not just preparation and training for later.
2   The whole child is considered to be important. Health, physical and mental, is emphasised, as well as the importance of feelings and thinking and spiritual aspects.
3   Learning is not compartmentalised, for everything links.
4   Intrinsic motivation resulting in child-initiated, self-directed activity, is valued.
5   Self-discipline is emphasised. (Points 4 and 5 relate to the child's autonomy.)
6   There are specially receptive periods of learning at different stages of development.
7   What children can do (rather than what they cannot do) is the starting point in the child's education.
8   There is an inner structure in a child which includes the imagination, and which can be encouraged by favourable conditions.
9   The people (both adults and children) with whom the child interacts are of central importance.
10 The child's education is seen as an interaction between the child and the environment the child is in, including in particular other people and knowledge itself.

The last principle can be expressed as a triangle involving three aspects of the curriculum – the child, the context, and the content. This is shown on the page opposite.

Links made with the National Curriculum (in England and Wales) or the 5–14 Guidelines (in Scotland) are best achieved through the Programmes of Study. Attainment Targets should never be the starting point, because they will not keep the curriculum in balance. When the curriculum becomes imbalanced, quality is no longer possible.

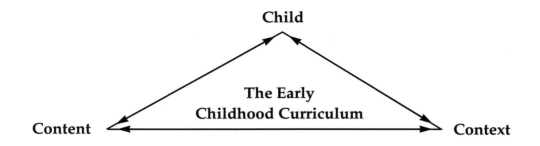

THE THREE C'S OF THE EARLY CHILDHOOD CURRICULUM

Child

**The Early
Childhood Curriculum**

Content

Context

What the child already knows

What the child needs to know

**What the child wants to know
more about**

**People, culture, race, gender,
special educational needs,
access, materials and physical
environment, outdoors, indoors,
places, events**

The three C's of the early childhood curriculum

In the next chapter, we shall look at examples of record-keeping in current use which espouse these principles.

3 Getting To Know What Other People Are Doing About Record-Keeping

Looking at how people in the past have approached record-keeping avoids re-inventing the wheel. So does looking at what people are doing now. The examples of record-keeping in this chapter are selected because we have direct contact with them and feel the importance of sharing them. We know there are many examples of good practice which we have not been able to include.

Parents At The Centre Of Record-Keeping

Let us begin with current practice, which continues in the tradition of our heritage, placing parents at the centre of good record-keeping. Jennifer Buckle, a Froebel trained teacher working in Devon with nursery classes and setting up playgroups, has developed a system of shared records with parents. We have included extracts rather than whole booklets, so that others can devise ones which are suitable for their own work setting. The first booklet is introduced to parents when Jennifer makes an initial home visit. The book is then left with them.

She has used a quotation from the Devon LEA booklet *Young Children Learning* (1990 p.28). 'A record should be a living document, should be continuous and used when appropriate.' The booklet also contains a statement of principles (Bruce, 1987). It has a section for the child to say what he or she does and also relates to areas such as health and language. This draws on *All about Me*, a book by Sheila Wolfendale. There are also excerpts from the TGAT Report (1988) on assessment and record-keeping, and from HMI documents.

Through a simple format, she packs in a mass of information and her thinking is shared. She includes examples of the type of record forms used in the school in which she works for recording progress in speaking, listening, reading, writing, marks, ethnology, science and personal development. Jennifer Buckle makes an initial home visit on school entry. She also invites parents to conferences in school through an appointment system, so that they can write the record together. This requires great commitment in order to free a member of staff to meet the parent during school-time.

Shared records

between home and school

by Jennifer Buckle

Our Nursery records of your child begin at the home visit when the dialogue between the home and school

begins, and the bonds between the family and the Nursery staff are started.

Information and books all about shared records are available around the Nursery for parents to enjoy. Obviously the records take time to fill in together while your child is attending the Nursery, so a convenient time for all of us needs to be arranged.

A record should be a living document and it should be continuous and used when appropriate.

There are many forms of record-keeping.

observations: samples of children's drawings. scribbles. paintings. etc. dated: photographs: tape recordings of language and communication: video recordings: scrapbook / diary between home and school: enabling children to participate in their own record-keeping: involving parents in open recording.

Observation

This is a major part of any assessment, as it is not just a passive, standing back activity. Observations should be of :- individual children, behaviour, interactions. Observations take place through :- working with an individual/group, conversations, watching a child in different situations.

In the science booklet, which is an example of a booklet made for parents to help them become more informed about the curriculum approach to particular subjects taught, she gives important messages. Science can be learnt out of doors as well as indoors, so the outdoors is very important. Children also need to be active learners, in real practical situations.

There are books on all the subjects of the curriculum. The science booklet which follows is given as an example of one of these. Each can be linked with the National Curriculum Programmes of Study (in England and Wales) or the 5–14 Guidelines (in Scotland). The science booklet also includes the science record form used in the school. Extracts from *Young Children Learning* by Devon LEA demonstrate that the school is linked with a wider network and does not work in isolation. Jennifer shows the importance of questions and dialogue, as well as parents working in the classroom. The booklet stresses nature, animals, insects, plants and the physical properties of matter, such as water and sand and how they introduce physics and chemistry. It also emphasises the science in cooking and household activities. In devising such booklets it is necessary to think what is important to share with parents, for example, in the teaching of science. The booklets help discussion, and may need to be made in a variety of languages.

The third booklet signals us that parents need to keep re-reading and borrowing booklets so that they gradually become more and more confident as the partnership develops. It emphasises the collaborative aspects of learning; the need to meet other adults and children, the learning involved in sharing, negotiating and co-operating as well as placing emphasis on creativity. It also shows how the work of the nursery, and the records kept, are useful to teachers later on as the child moves into school, introducing the notion of continuity with progression, and quietly dispelling any idea that children just play in the nursery, or that real learning only comes later on.

At a parents' evening the work of the nursery is again shared, and there is the opportunity for parents to meet, so that a feeling of the school as a community is encouraged. The booklets and charts are always displayed in the class at child height for both children and adults to browse through. Parents are also invited to an open-evening in the school after the initial home visits are made, where the booklets are displayed and explained. These are constantly available for loan, as the sharing of information is an ongoing and continual process. As the books are placed at child level the children are part of the process.

Science

by Jennifer Buckle

Has planted seeds
and watched them grow.

Some children learn more effectively
outside .... garden, pond, sand,
water, digging, plants, mini-beasts
and other animals.

Welcome to

our Nursery

By Jennifer Buckle

In the Nursery the children enjoy the fun of playing together, making friends and learning to share and to co-operate with others. Junior pupils also work with us each day.

If young children are encouraged to use creative materials, this will help their writing and reading later. They enjoy making marks, scribbling and drawing . . . .

and they enjoy making a mess!

At each session, the children have a snack at their 'cafe' when they help to prepare the food and serve each other. In this photograph they have enjoyed the gooseberry jam that they made last week.

Assessment and record keeping are an important part of the educational process, and this will start at the Home visit. Our shared Records enable a dialogue between home and school, sharing and understanding together the needs of your child.

These records will also help the Infant teachers to know what your child can achieve.

We need and value help from
parents and our school welcomes
every family to take part in
all aspects of school life.
The children in the Nursery join
infant storytime, assemblies, all
celebrations and enjoy swimming
and sports facilities.

Our Toy Library is open every week in term time, so that all families can borrow games to enjoy together at home.

Jen Cartwright and Jan Savage (formerly Primary Adviser and Advisory Teacher respectively in Devon LEA) disseminated Jennifer's shared record-keeping with parents, at a multi-professional conference on early childhood education and care in January 1992. This was attended by those working in playgroups, day nurseries, child minding, family centres, nursery and reception classes. The conference, much appreciated by those attending, took up the recommendations of the 'Starting with Quality' Report 1990 including the assertion that every institution should keep records.

The whole child

Sheila Wolfendale's *All About Me* record, often adapted, has influenced those working in a number of fields. Again, this keeps the tradition of involving parents from the start, and emphasises physical development, health, feelings, and relationships and language, rather than only subject knowledge such as mathematics. For this reason, it makes a useful antidote to the potential domination of the subject-based concerns in the National Curriculum. It reminds us that we are working with the whole child, not just intellectual aspects (Bruce, 1987 Principle 2).

A backcloth for our record-keeping

A different kind of resource, is what we might call the 'Backcloth Book' such as Mary Sheridan's classics *From Birth to Five Years* (1973) and *Spontaneous Play in Early Childhood* (1977). They remind us of the links between development and learning and (1973) that parents hope to be given 'truthful explanation' of their child's progress. Martin Hughes' research (1990, 1991) indicates that this is what parents want more than anything else when they meet professionals. Mary Sheridan stresses (1973) that when parents say for example, they do not think their child is hearing, they are 'usually right.' When parents are concerned about literacy or maths, for example, we must listen and work together. The Royal National Institute for the Blind (RNIB) has developed a booklet for parents and those working with young multi-handicapped visually-impaired children which helps to give an understanding of these areas, (HMSO, 1993).

Although it would be unwise to use the charts in Mary Sheridan's books, or the ideas in the RNIB book in rigid ways, they are useful as 'Backcloth Books' in monitoring children's progress.

Alice Honig's (1984) image that we particularly need to help children with

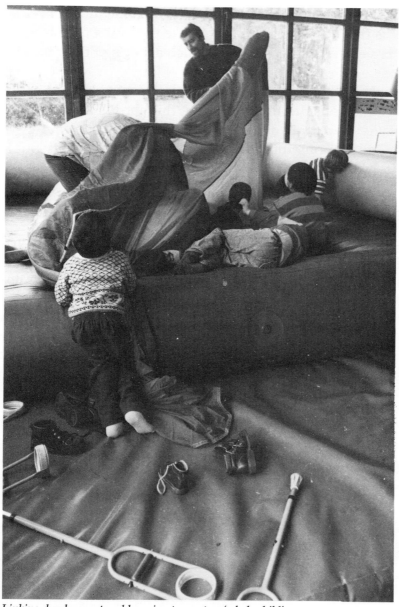

Linking development and learning to create a 'whole child'

special educational needs to 'dance the development ladder' is useful. Learning depends on general development.

Reviewing – must it be a written record?

The Pre-School Playgroups Association booklet (*What Children Learn in Playgroup*, 1991) gives a wealth of ideas on managing and organising stimulating provision for young children. Perhaps the most important assertion in the booklet is that adults must (p.71) 'make time on a regular basis to discuss how far they have been successful and which aspects of their work they need to review or revise.'

This links what is offered to children with the way children act on what is offered. We need to consider to what extent this should be written down, and to what extent it should remain a verbal review. This has been at the forefront of discussion not only among the staff at Redford House Nursery but for all who work in similarly busy settings.

Can we overdo the writing down of evaluation?

In Chapter 2 we look at the possibility that we might overdo the writing down of a child's development and learning through rigidly pre-structuring our observations in ways which in the end give us less information. The same problem can apply where evaluation is concerned. There are dangers attached to writing down in advance too much about material provision, or in planning too far ahead. The Early Years Curriculum Group (EYCG), 1989 warned against

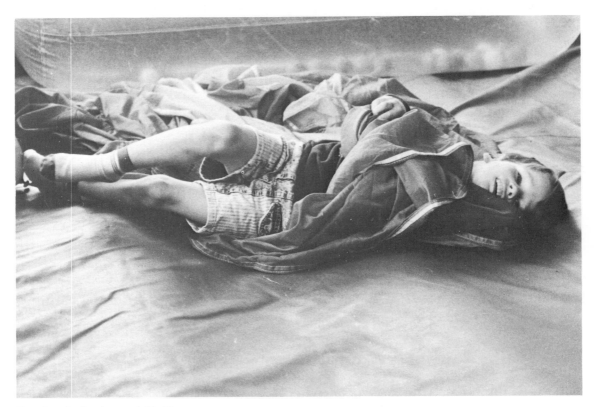

Dancing the developmental ladder

pre-structured programmes through which children are determinedly taken. Remember Tim and the Roman Project (see p.21).

The making of long-term plans needs to be more in the spirit of Wynne Harlen's *Possible Lines of Direction* (1982). PLOD, see also, Bruce (1987) on 'Evaluation and Assessment'.

MAKING ORGANIC AND FLEXIBLE LONG-TERM PLANS

Record-keeping needs to be a continuing dialogue between long-term plans and the individual child's development and learning day by day and week by week. Incidental and spontaneous learning events can then be incorporated into long-term plans. This enriches the original plan. We could call this 'organic long-term planning'. Allenby Nursery, in Southall, (London Borough of Ealing) has tried to make long-term plans which have a sense of direction without a rigid pre-structured programme or set project, using Chapter 8 *Time to Play* (Bruce 1991).

At Allenby Nursery staff acted on their observations of children and made a display of books, which led to talk of maps initiated by the children's response to the Indian Fairy Tale of 'The Six Blind Men and the Elephant', and the problems of finding the way to the next village. *The Zoo* and a walk to the Post Office again raised the need for a map.

This resulted in an explosion of interest in maps, also encouraged by postcards arriving from children on holiday in Kenya, Ireland and Canada. These locations were marked on a wall map. Picture maps and road signs were found in various stories, such as *Goldilocks*, *The Gingerbread Man*, *Five Bears Go to the Seaside*. A photograph book of the neighbourhood was made showing road signs and printed words in the environment.

A map of the nursery garden was constructed as a story prop for *We're going on a Treasure Hunt, I wonder what we'll Find*, requiring the use of sequence and direction; oral and listening skills; prepositions, and adverts.

The staff capitalised on the children's interest and encouraged the map-making.

Gurpreet, (aged three years and eight-months) removed a diary from her mother's bag at home and told her in Punjabi that there was a map on the inside page. Her mother was very excited, and told the nursery staff. She came into nursery and found a book with a world map. She drew a representation of

Spontaneous learning can be incorporated into long-term plans

Kenya, which is where her grandmother lives. (She had previously only represented people.) Her mother says she is constantly finding and referring to maps.

Michael, (aged four years and one month) brought a map of his garden to school which identified the boundary fence, the kitchen window, the pond (actually a bowl of water) and the grass.

Aiden (aged four years and seven months) made lots of treasure maps of the nursery garden, marking features such as the sand pit and climbing equipment. He also included directional arrows.

The long-term chart was continually added to in the light of the individual child's needs. Details of a child's connection with the long-term plan were noted in the child's individual profile and folder of work. (See the Allenby Nursery Shared Activities chart on the next page.)

Staff at Pen Green Family Centre, Corby, Northamptonshire, have developed a 'possible lines of development chart' which they call PLOD, into which they have integrated their observations of the children's schemas. The PLOD chart shows possible lines of development for Kari whose Piagetian schemas (see Glossary) include a strong fascination with rotation, and loves things that go round and round, as well as for Alex who loves bike wheels and turning lids. At Pen Green, links are made with the National Curriculum through the programmes of study on the individual child records, as well as with the schemas as a way of focusing observations after they are made. These are kept in the large box-files open to the child's parents. Parents are introduced to the nursery with home visits by their family worker, when the entry form, parent and staff observation sheet, and the Pen Green schema booklet for parents are explained. Once children start in the nursery, the parents continue to help staff with observations and record-keeping on specially devised forms. Examples of children's work with photographs are kept in a folder as well as in the child's own book. Children help to decide what will be in their books and adults write for them when necessary. In this way adults, staff, parents and children make the book together. When children leave, the records kept will link with the Northamptonshire LEA *First Focus Booklet*. The child's book is a parent-held record, which is shown to the receiving teachers by the child and parents. The PLOD forms which relate to the child are also sent to the school showing what curriculum content has been covered. Examples from significant on-the-spot specimen records are also shown to the school. The main receiving school and parents are delighted with the system. Parents have the pleasure of the modern equivalent of a baby biography (see Chapter 2). The primary school has invaluable information which can be put to good use in planning the next step

SUMMER TERM - IDEAS FOR SHARED ACTIVITIES

LANGUAGE EXTENSION
- Stories read in Home Languages and English
- Allenby Environment - photographs
- Road Safety language
- Use tape recorder for childrens' voices
- Garden: observing, predicting e.g. 'What will happen next?'
- Rhyming words
See language also under cookery

LITERACY
Involve parents and students materials, year 3 children in Home Language Story.
- Traditional stories 'Little Red Hen', 'Enormous turnip', 'Goldilocks', 'Meg and Mogs Garden', 'Hare and Tortoise', 'Jim and the Beanstalk', 'Jack and the Beanstalk', 'Six Blind Men and the Elephant', 'The Hat Maker', 'Meg and Mogs Veg', 'Peter and the Wolf', 'The Teddy Bears Picnic', 'The Bear Hunt'
- Letter-writing 'Dear Zoo' (Dual language text)
- Drawing books
- Maintaining care of all books
- Develop listening skills at story time
- Encourage children to behave like teachers

SOCIAL + EMOTIONAL DEVELOPMENT
- Visit Post Office
- Tidy-Up Time, encourage children to look at books if they don't tidy up
- Caring for books

HUMANITIES
Allenby environment - mapping/road signs/print

CELEBRATIONS
Afro-caribbean party, parents to attend birthdays of individual children

CREATIVE
- Junk - castle building/road or house building
- Book making
- Seed-pressing into Plasticine
- Seaside collage
- Range of blues, yellows, greens, red etc.

COOKERY
- Bread making ('Little Red Hen')
- Turnip soup ('Tale of the Turnip')
- Porridge ('Three Bears') ('Salty, sweet, lumpy, hot, cold')

SCIENCE
- Planting cuttings and seeds, potatoes, sunflowers, tomatoes, beans in tyres in garden
Also herbs which smell - 'Butterfly' bush (Buddleia), Plant colour – Coriander Mint, Methi, Chick peas, Lavender
Snails - Encouraging observation and prediction in the garden
Rubbish/litter/conservation - Weather.

TECHNOLOGY
- Books - threading, folding, concertina
- Bookmarks
- Book binding
- Printing paper covers
- Make books of 'collections' e.g. shoes, clothes, watches, toys etc.
- Display of books + posters

MATHS
- Make water play (and sand play) word mobiles – wet, trickle, bubble, gurgle, clear, glisten, sparkle, splash, drip, droplets, glitter, splatter
- Story language: 'Once upon a time' 'One day'
- Tenses: past, present, future
- Days of the week
- Time: long, short
- Growing words: high, tall, long, short, shorter than, thin

DISPLAYS
- Root vegetables
- Snails, tadpoles and frogs (briefly)
- Afro-caribbean celebration
- Seaside- Books - traditional stories

MUSIC + RHYMES
- 'Goldilocks and three bears', 'Postman Pat', 'There was a princess long ago'
- Mary, Mary quite contrary
- We are going to plant a bean
- Titch
- 'Teddy Bears Picnic'
- 'Peter and the Wolf'.

VISITS
- To a library, Post Office, local shops

Visits from
Parcel force, post person

BOOKS

Ideas for shared activities from Allenby Nursery

for the child's learning. More details of Pen Green's approach to record-keeping can be found in *Learning to be Strong* by Margy Whalley (1993).

Although the chart (on page 48) begins with Kari's and Alex's educational needs, it will also help other children to learn. We do not need to make a long-term planning chart for every child. Athey (1990 p.30) writes 'unreflective child centredness has led to the false belief that every child requires a unique educational programme. Constructivist teachers know that many children share similar cognitive concerns.' Using long-term planning charts which are of a flexible, organic, growing nature, plans can be carried through in ways which suit the children. Individuals can be catered for, and particular areas of knowledge are introduced. The box-files link with the PLOD charts, and so assessment and evaluation are inter-woven.

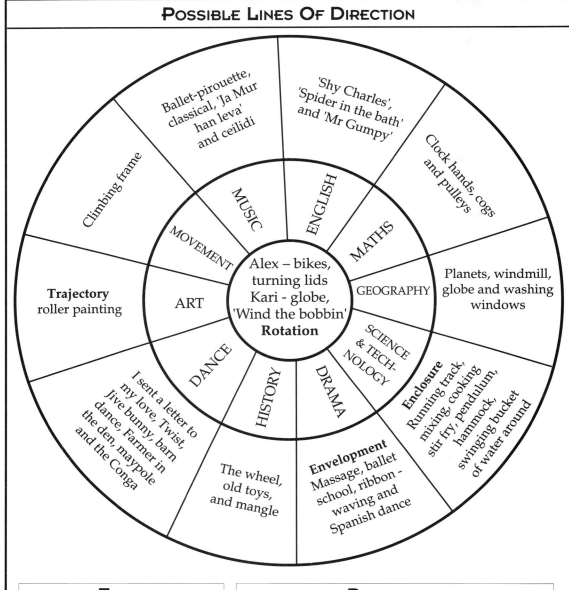

POSSIBLE LINES OF DIRECTION

(Center) Alex – bikes, turning lids Kari - globe, 'Wind the bobbin' **Rotation**

Inner ring: MUSIC · ENGLISH · MOVEMENT · MATHS · ART · GEOGRAPHY · DANCE · SCIENCE & TECH-NOLOGY · HISTORY · DRAMA

Outer ring:
- Ballet-pirouette, classical, 'Ja Mur han leva' and ceilidi
- 'Shy Charles', 'Spider in the bath' and 'Mr Gumpy'
- Clock hands, cogs and pulleys
- Climbing frame
- Planets, windmill, globe and washing windows
- **Trajectory** roller painting
- **Enclosure** Running track, mixing, cooking, stir fry, pendulum, hammock, swinging bucket of water around
- I sent a letter to my love, Twist, Jive bunny, barn dance, Farmer in the den, maypole and the Conga
- The wheel, old toys, and mangle
- **Envelopment** Massage, ballet school, ribbon - waving and Spanish dance

TRIPS
Sywell Airport, station, windmill, water wheel, fair, Kettering Museum and Rockingham Triangle (track)

RESOURCES
Globe (with relief), gyroscope, balls, balloons, record-player, potter's wheel, cement mixer, washing machine, fair, catherine wheels, kaleidoscope, spinning top, plugholes, big mixer (in kitchen), windmills, pencil sharpener, pulleys, tyres, hula hoops, humming top, Victorian theatre toy and telescope

Possible Lines of Direction (PLOD). Specially devised forms from Pen Green

ANGELA'S GROUP **MONTH BEGINNING** ....

Name of child	Trajectory	Rotation	Enclosure	Enveloping	Infilling	Transporting	Core and Radial	Other
Steven	✓	✓		✓		✓		
Lynda		✓				✓		
Jacob		✓	✓		✓	✓		
John	✓	✓			✓			
Zach	✓					✓		
Stacey	✓				✓	✓		
Robert				✓		✓		
James	✓			✓				
Clare				✓				
Lydia	✓		✓			✓		

Specially devised form from Pen Green

CONTINUOUS ASSESSMENT RECORD

Name of Child   Date

Place   Time

Length of time   Alone

Group - who is in it?

How did the child get involved?

What happened?

What does the play/investigation seem to be about?

Schemas?

LINKS TO NATIONAL CURRICULUM PROGRAMMES OF STUDY

English	Maths	Science	Tech.	Geog.
History	Dance	Art	Music	Drama
Movement				

Observed by:

Specially devised form from Pen Green

Area	Plan	Children		Staff	Outings
Corridor	Magnets travelling along string Den Stories Self select construction	Kirsten Jacob Keith Leanne Clare James	Trajectory Transporting Scatter	Cath Cath Jackie	Zoe Laura Natalie Katey Washing windows
Wet Area	Rotary whisks Other whisks { Containers Chocolate powder } Clear bottles Salt Flour shaker Pasta Oil Powder paint (to add colour) Thursday – mashed Cooked dough potatoes	Robert John Kimberly Jacob Natalie Zoe Craig Joely	Rotation Envelopment In + out	Lucy Carmen a.m. Jackie p.m. Carmen	
Work-shop	Playing with string Cats cradle Tin can stilts * Add glue and bits	Jacob Robert Thomas	Connection Enclosure	Sarah Linds	Resources Cans, strings, pestle + mortar, squeegy, chamois
Drawing	Train set self-service Nice floor - silver + gold * Repeat	Mark Joely Daniel	Connection Trajectory Enclosure	Tracy	
Café	Veg, fruit + toast	Alex	Trajectory	Becky a.m. Rie p.m.	
Home Corner	Chopping vegetables			Chris	
Low Ceiling	a.m. clear for dentist p.m. large rolls of paper 1/10/92 rolls of paper for wrapping children block jungle. Repeat	Joanne Craig Natalie Grant	Envelopment	Cath	
Writing	Calculator, envelope Pritt Stick, scissors * Repeat	Joely Kari Jannice B.	On top Envelopment Dab		
Outside	Buckets, sponges, brushes Pulleys, buckets, gravel, sand & sawdust, paper Bikes with trailers Cornflower on large table Parachute Rolls of paper Different kinds of measures	Kerry John M. James H. Aaron Zoe Thomas Natalie Stephen Steven Alex James Jacob	Envelopment Transporting Trajectory Rotation	Lucy	

Specially devised form from Pen Green

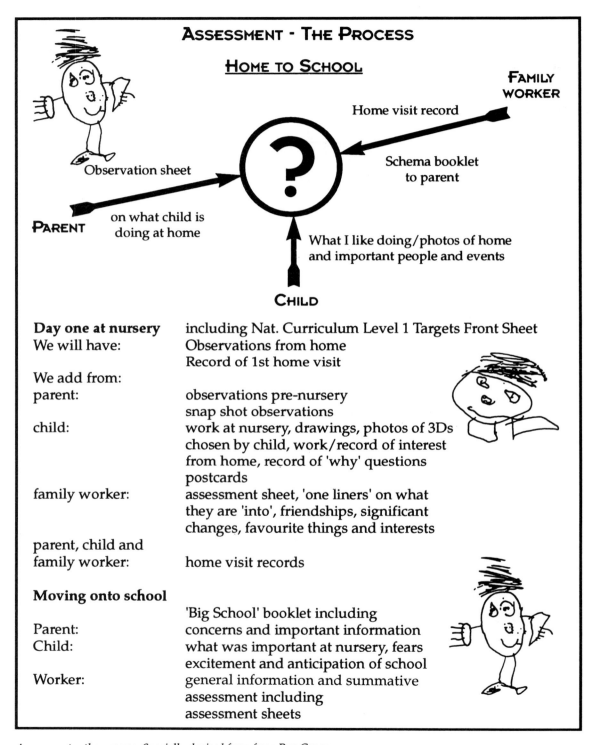

ASSESSMENT - THE PROCESS

HOME TO SCHOOL

FAMILY WORKER

Home visit record

Schema booklet to parent

Observation sheet

PARENT

on what child is doing at home

What I like doing/photos of home and important people and events

CHILD

Day one at nursery We will have:	including Nat. Curriculum Level 1 Targets Front Sheet Observations from home Record of 1st home visit
We add from: parent:	observations pre-nursery snap shot observations
child:	work at nursery, drawings, photos of 3Ds chosen by child, work/record of interest from home, record of 'why' questions postcards
family worker:	assessment sheet, 'one liners' on what they are 'into', friendships, significant changes, favourite things and interests
parent, child and family worker:	home visit records
Moving onto school	
Parent:	'Big School' booklet including concerns and important information
Child:	what was important at nursery, fears excitement and anticipation of school
Worker:	general information and summative assessment including assessment sheets

Assessment – the process. Specially devised form from Pen Green

ANGELA'S GROUP	MONTH BEGINNING 15/9/92
Name of child	Interests
Steven	friendships, rotation, hats, bikes, soft room, pulleys, snacks, mini-bus
Lynda	collecting things, friends, what people are doing, stories, dough, siblings, mini-bus
Jacob	string, climbing trees, fishing rods, how things work, pulleys, mixing, books – 'Don't put mustard in the custard.'
John	diggers, train set, duplo cars, animals, dinosaurs, books, water, mini-bus
Zach	water, bikes, friends, making models, homecorner, soft room
Stacey	small threading, tree house, bikes, homecorner
Robert	cutting string, hats, capes, bikes, homecorner, softroom, other groups, mixing, friends
James	rocking horse, flopsy, stickers, slide, water
Clare	washing hands, playdough, writing area, snacks, flushing ('flushing the loo')
Lydia	water, high heels, special box, changing clothes, outside, staff, the buggy

Specially devised form from Pen Green

The tradition of using modern research and theory to enrich record-keeping

In the last chapter, we saw Susan Isaacs use the psychodynamic theory available to her to make child records and to evaluate the curriculum.

Staff at Pen Green have used Piagetian schemas as an integral part of their record-keeping. This work was initiated by Chris Athey in the Froebel Nursery Research Project of 1972–77. Victoria Hurst and Tina Bruce (Early Years Curriculum Group (EYCG) 1989) demonstrated a curriculum planning web based on the Piagetian schemas (inside and outside) arising from observations of children in a particular class, and linking with the National Curriculum. Unless topic planning is based on observations of children it tends to put children through a pre-structured programme. Remember Tim and the Romans (see pp.21 and 43). Pen Green's topic was based on observations of Kari's schemas. The long-term plan linked with his box-file which demonstrates his interest in trajectories.

It is important to remember that staff at Allenby, (a nursery class in a primary school) Redford House Nursery, (a workplace nursery) and Pen Green Family Centre have participated in courses which have helped them to understand and feel relaxed about the theory they are using. Parents have also attended. This has helped everyone working with the child to see the difference between advance planning through the pre-structured topic approach and advance planning based on observation of the child, such as PLOD.

Working towards shared principles, shared theory and shared practice through record-keeping

An essential part of working as a team of staff is to develop shared principles. Sometimes staff with a variety of approaches come together, and need to tease out a common approach, so that practice is not confused, contradictory, or condemning of each other's work, and poor (Lally 1991).

Joyce French, headteacher of Bridlington Nursery School, Humberside, has taken the approach traditionally used by nursery nurses in record-keeping, known as PIES (physical, intellectual, emotional and social development). In this way, she could begin to look at record-keeping with her staff, using what is familiar and understood. She and the staff have developed dated daily sheets on which they observe 'significance through learning materials'. For example, Josh, aged three, was observed connecting tubes together at the water tray. There is also space on the sheet to write down what learning opportunities are to be offered as a follow-up to the observation. The follow-ups come under the

CURRICULUM - THE ADULT'S JOB IS TO PLAN, PREPARE AND ORGANISE AN EDUCATIONAL ENVIRONMENT BASED ON THE CHILD'S DEVELOPING NEEDS

SOCIAL DEVELOPMENT
- To develop communication skills - children learn to talk by talking, (use open-ended questions and those that require more than a yes/no answer)
- To enable child to interact with peer group
- To encourage a sense of responsibility
- To help children to interact with adults

EMOTIONAL DEVELOPMENT
- To encourage children to express feelings
- To develop each individual child's self-esteem and a sense of achievement
- To provide a secure environment
- To develop confidence
- To enable children to cope with fears, anxieties and difficult experiences

DEVELOPMENT OF THE YOUNG CHILD

PHYSICAL DEVELOPMENT
- To develop manipulative skills
- To provide opportunities for children to gain control over their own bodies N.B. large movements come before finer movements
- To develop hand/eye co-ordination.

INTELLECTUAL DEVELOPMENT
- To enable young children to grasp basic maths and science concepts and problem solving in all areas
- To develop language and reasoning skills
- To encourage learning through direct experience
- To develop concentration and literacy skills
- To encourage creativity and use of imagination
- To develop observational skills

Pies Form, developed by Joyce French, Humberside

headings: skills, concepts and knowledge, which are again familiar to the staff and link with the local authority's requirements as well as those of the National Curriculum or Piagetian schema. The staff have created a framework for record-keeping which helps them to work together without constraining what they do with the children and their families. It is easily shared with parents. Staff at Redford House have taken up the PIES approach and added language development to it – PLIES; (see Chapter 4).

In this chapter so far, we have looked at a variety of ways of advance planning which are in keeping with the principles of early childhood education, and yet can be linked easily with the National Curriculum or 5–14 Guidelines.

User-friendly record-keeping

A number of people have recently been plotting children's progress onto charts with concrete images such as jigsaws, flowers and houses. Bradford's 'Assessing Children at the Start of School', the Barnet Record, the Hammersmith and Fulham Nursery and Primary Record, and the Merton Process Record, avoid using concrete images but they are also user-friendly. As well as being user-friendly, all of these approaches use *aides-mémoire* and prompts rather than check-lists. They give a bottom up, rather than top down link with the National Curriculum.

Bradford LEA – assessing children at the start of school
This stresses that 'parents and carers, as the first educators, should be given the opportunity and time to contribute information to staff about their child's experiences and achievements within their own family and community cultures'. It also emphasises the importance of bilingual adults to ensure that 'the assessment of bilingual children is full and accurate' (p.5). It advocates that (p.7)

> *observations will need to be made during the normal course of classroom activities, and will aim, over a period of time, to give a full picture of the child working across a range of curriculum areas, in individual and group settings.*

It suggests prompts which bring together the National Curriculum subjects and the HMI areas of experience. Sheila Wolfendale's *All About Me* has influenced suggestions for the child's, parents' or carers' contribution to the record.

> *The prompts are intended to guide and not prescribe the observations. They are not a definitive list but may assist staff in the recordings of their observations.*

This approach to record-keeping ensures that throughout a child's time in school, there is a consistent approach grounded in sound educational principles.

The Barnet Record

This approach also adheres strongly to the principles of early childhood education. The record is aimed at structuring observations to promote understanding, planning, and sharing insights with colleagues and parents.

The record uses prompt sheets, but these are not tick-lists or headings to place observations in a straitjacket. As we saw in Chapter 2, Ann Alderman, (formerly General Inspector, Early Years Education, and currently Advisory Officer for the Children Act) views these as dangerous. The first section suggests lists of information to be gathered on first meeting parents. Teachers and nursery nurses are encouraged to have a pocket book or self-adhesive ('stick-it') notelets for easy transfer to the child's file, after coding the observation (as at Wessex Gardens). This is very much in the spirit of the on-the-spot record recommended in Chapter 2, where adults make on-the-spot observations of what the child does and says in a particular situation and context. The code acts as a resource for observation, helping reflection on areas such as creativity, imagination, co-ordination and motor skills, language and literacy, social and emotional development, knowledge and understanding. The dated and coded observation is then thought about in terms of action to be taken and links with the planning file containing advanced plans for displays, stories etc.

Particular children are targeted each week. There is a further form on which to make a termly or half-termly review. This summarises the child's development and determines what action should be taken. The sampling of dated children's work in a large folder is stressed, as in the Primary Learning Record, the Merton Process Record, or the Hammersmith and Fulham Nursery Record. Photographs help to keep records of three-dimensional work or dances or drama. Tapes keep records of language and music. These should be analysed and the comment labelled on the sample at the time. A personal scrapbook recording details such as activities and particular interests can also be kept by the child and accompany him/her on entry to school.

The Barnet Record is widely used in the borough, yet each school uses it uniquely. It is user-friendly, soundly based on the principles of early childhood education and can be linked with the future records, which will need to lay more emphasis on the National Curriculum as the child enters statutory schooling. It is flexible and appropriate in a variety of settings.

At Hampden Way, nursery staff have reviewed their work with parents and reaffirmed their priority of further strengthening an already sound partnership.

This will be facilitated through such a method of record-keeping. At Holly Park, the reception class and nursery class work together. In September, the reception class teacher works in the nursery, making notes, observing, and introducing children to the reception area in small groups prior to January. This enables the nursery teacher to make home visits, as well as the nursery nurse. It is an example of excellent practice in helping children to make good transitions, as well as an example of good record-keeping.

At Moss Hall staff are supported and reaffirmed in their philosophy through the Barnet Record. Here, the 'stick-it' type label is used to great effect. In spite of a senior staff member being on maternity leave, records and comments on progress, with action to be taken in the termly reviews she left for colleagues, are proving invaluable.

St. Catherine's and Wessex Gardens are nursery classes in primary schools. At St. Catherine's, the teacher builds her observations of Max using 'stick-it' labels and later that day writing the code beside it. The 'action' section is as full as the basic observation. When he is new, his friendship with Nati is noted six days into starting at the nursery. Both can speak Spanish. Spanish is valued and the teacher invites Max's mother to read *Spot* to the class in Spanish. By January, he plays co-operatively in a group of children using Spanish and English, and still likes to be in the home corner. He is encouraged to visit the pond daily and makes a book about frogs to link with his love of drawing and emergent writing and stories. Some junk modelling materials are brought in which inspire him to make models of frogs too. We see his new learning unfolding. We see what the teacher does about it. At Wessex Gardens, the teacher uses a system of colour-coded highlighting pens to enhance her observations. She skilfully shares her observations with parents and has a comfortable sofa in the classroom which helps to create a relaxed atmosphere, a necessary backcloth to focused and valuable dialogue between home and school. The atmosphere created by this teacher and her colleagues is such that parents feel confident that they are receiving 'truthful explanation' of their child's progress in a spirit of real partnership.

In these five Barnet schools, the excellent early years practice was enhanced by the Barnet Nursery Record. It is built upon, when children enter their primary schools, using the booklet *Entry Profiling; a Framework for Developing a Policy* which stresses that whilst teachers are initially getting to know children, observations need to be built of the children's actions and play in spontaneous situations. This is a continuous process which will gradually link into the Barnet Primary Record. The booklet has been developed by the Advisory Teacher for Early Years and the Advisory Teacher for Assessment.

The Primary Learning Record

This keeps the principles of development and learning valued in this book, and yet links with the content focus of the National Curriculum in acceptable and valuable ways. It began as a language and literacy record, (1990 p.36) but states 'as well as recording the children's language development it has already been providing a way of mapping children's learning across the curriculum'. It became the Primary Learning Record so that parents/teacher discussion and child conferences are included in relation to English, Mathematics and Science in the National Curriculum. Check-lists are eschewed, but through the use of an *aide mémoire* on the record, observations can be focused to consider particular subjects. The Primary Learning Record helps parents and adults working with children (1990 p.38) 'in making observations, gathering evidence of progress, reflecting on the evidence and using it for forward planning'.

If we look again at the three C's making up the curriculum (the child, the context, the content) in order to consider all aspects that our records must cover, we see that the Primary Learning Record is strong in every respect. More than any other record, it has highlighted the need to look at context in providing fuller access to the curriculum.

The Merton Process Record

This, like the Bradford Assessment Record, the Barnet Record, and the Primary Learning Record, sees record-keeping as an integral part of the whole approach to the curriculum.

Merton LEA worked with RIHE (now Roehampton Institute) over several years, encouraging schools to participate, but with no compulsion to do so. It is now widely valued in the borough. The borough recognises that there will always be the need to provide regular courses to initiate new staff into the approach to record-keeping as well as reaffirming the principles under-pinning this style of record-keeping. Staff at both Pen Green Family Centre and Redford House Nursery also use regular in-service training as part of their record-keeping process.

The Merton records are kept in user-friendly hardbacked booklets of a handy size to rest on laps, or table-tops. The processes of learning and working with children are valued as much as the products of the learning. This means that the check-list approach is discouraged, and instead there are prompts in the form of headings on easily referred to flaps which extend to both sides of the paper and loosely guide and focus observations of the child. Record-keepers are discouraged from writing under the headings as this would be a straitjacket, like a check-list. Prompts include interaction, attitude, problem solving, representation. The on-the-spot specimen record approach is encouraged through the use of dotted lines which can be ignored by those who prefer blank paper (like the authors of this book and most of the participants in the Froebel Block Play Research Project, 1992). This means that the booklets are very accessible, can be used flexibly and idiosyncratically, and yet are sufficiently uniform and standardised. A separate page is used for each observation on each child. These can be collected under one child's profile every half term or so, to ensure that no child is neglected. The borough stresses that these notebooks are just that – notebooks. They are not formal records and so do not require neat handwriting.

They are owned and belong to the record-keeper. Record-keepers can also use highlight pens to colour code the notes if this seems helpful to them. In other words, these notebooks emphasise the importance of process as well as products. They continue the valuable tradition of specimen records, and child study which is both retrospective and prospective. They thus inform planning, organisation and management of the curriculum, both for children in general and individuals. They show *how* children learn as well as *what* they learn. The record-keeping can focus observations.

At the moment, teachers keep these records, but nursery nurses are joining in as the pilot stage is completed and parents may also want to keep notebooks. The Merton Process approach has a parent-discussion record, designed to support and structure meetings with parents initiated by school staff. Some schools operate a home-visiting scheme, but in order to have a uniform approach throughout the borough, a parent discussion is held at or near the point of entry. Inset training enables staff to establish a partnership with parents. It is important to stress the in-service training in using the Merton Process booklets. This comprises two days and five twilight sessions, and the course runs each academic year to initiate or refresh. Just as those using Piagetian schema observation in their record-keeping, for example at Pen Green or Redford House, need in-service training, so do those using this approach.

The Merton Process notebooks reflect the philosophy of early childhood education and need to be understood from that perspective. There are no short cuts to good record-keeping. Again and again we come to see that records reflect our philosophy and our theories of how children learn. The parent-discussion notebook also creates in an informal way, a baseline of where the child is on entry to the nursery. The record links with the summative conference with the parents, when the child leaves the nursery to enter the main school. Since confidential issues may emerge, it is important that parents agree what goes into the summative record. For this, three different instances of learning are selected from the observation notebook. The summative record is designed to give a vignette of the child and analysis of learning to date through these examples. There is also space for the next steps to be taken.

This is important in terms of continuity with progression, as the child leaves the nursery and enters the main school. It facilitates the introduction of the National Curriculum through firm partnership with parents who will have become accustomed to seeing staff taking notes during conversations, without this detracting from genuine discussion. Through an atmosphere of trust on both sides, they will share the process of summing up.

RECORDS OF ACHIEVEMENT

The Hammersmith and Fulham LEA Nursery Record of Achievement links with the Primary Record of Achievement, which is based on it, but obviously lays more emphasis on the National Curriculum. It reiterates the principles of good record-keeping in its objectives. These are that:

1   *The record of achievement should contain information about the progress of the child in all areas of development. It should relate to the National Curriculum and the LEA curriculum statement, but should also reflect the broad, play-based curriculum special to the early years.*
2   *The information should be the summation of all running records of the child's performance. It should not be necessary to arrange extra assessment activities.*
3   *The record of achievement is supported by evidence which includes samples of work, photographs or sketches of practical work, records of teacher/pupil discussions, observations of the child's activities.*
4   *It should be an open record discussed with parents before the child moves to the next class.*
5   *Pupils should be involved in identifying selected evidence of achievement and, where possible, in planning for their own learning.*

The first page gives background information for example, on first language and health. The second page gives cross-curricular learning. Headings in this section are 'approaches to learning including communication skills, problem solving, ability to plan work and evaluate it, use of time, persistence' and 'knowledge across the curriculum including awareness of environmental issues, health issues, social issues.' The next page gives language and literacy, mathematics, science and technology headings with prompts to help focus examples given from the running records.

The last page gives creative areas of learning, physical achievement, teachers' comments and parents' comments. For example, the notes for Fionn (aged four) under the heading 'approaches to learning ...' read:

> *Logical approach to problems e.g. when asked to tidy up a table littered with sequins, 'If I put all these sequins in a little pile, they'll be easier to pick up. I know if I sweep them all together, I can pick them up in one handful'. Then went on to get a piece of paper on which to sweep them over the side of the table so that he could easily pour them back into the dish. Concentrates well – able to work under his own steam, making decisions about what he is going to do. Able to solve complex jigsaw puzzles and block designs. Asks questions, looks and thinks.*

The teacher writes of Jade (aged four) from the 'approaches to learning ...' section of the record:

> *Jade learns most of her skills by watching other people. She was always shy about asking questions and to compensate for this, her observation skills are excellent, e.g. 19.9.91 was observed watching a child making a model of a person and copying that child's model. Also see observation enclosed for 23.3.92 which gives a picture of her attitude towards her work. She is industrious and careful about her work. She concentrates for long periods e.g. observation on 17.2.92: she spends half an hour at a matching game, watching first, then participating. She frequently evaluates her work – you can see her standing back to look at it, and then she makes changes.*

Connor (aged four) has the following notes on the first page under dietary restrictions:

> *Chocolate/cocoa. Needs monumental amount of encouragement to eat normal food – bird like portions. Connor can detect one sliver of cabbage hidden in a forkful of mashed potatoes!*

Under 'approaches to learning ...', the record says:

> *Connor's lack of confidence makes him a bit tentative to approaching new activities – he needs adult encouragement to be drawn into different/novel situations – he loves things that are familiar e.g. he knows all about dinosaurs and feels very secure when holding forth about them. His approach to learning is in fact a bit like his approach to strange food – he is highly suspicious and wary. The areas he chooses most in the nursery are: book corner, outside, sand/water, puzzle table and occasionally drawing/painting.*

The teacher comments:

> *Connor has always been very appreciative of the nursery and forthcoming with compliments – he has a great sense of humour and treasures memories of things that have pleased him and often refers back 'do you remember that time when you tricked us?' It has been lovely having him as part of our group, and we are all sorry that he is leaving so early, just as he is about to blossom.*

The parent comments:

> *I think that this report does reflect Connor accurately. I know he is a child who needs lots of encouragement to attempt new things. Hopefully he will 'blossom' at his new school.*

Connor's parents did not want him to go to school so soon, but the receiving Church school said he would lose his place if he did not take it then. Uprooting flourishing children out of nursery and putting them into infant classes at a very young age cuts across continuity with progression.

Shahrazad (aged four) hears Arabic spoken at home and on visits to Algeria, but English is her first language. In the 'knowledge across the curriculum...' section of the record, under 'environment' the teacher has written:

> *Knows about not picking the plants in the garden. Helps to water plants and is fiercely protective of snails, ladybirds, woodlice etc.*

She then writes under the 'science' heading:

> *Fascinated by woodlice, snails, worms, ladybirds, but does not like to handle them. Enjoys activities that involve mixing ingredients together and observing changes e.g. making dough, cooking, dissolving things like salt, sugar etc. Able to distinguish elementary properties of objects and sort and classify accordingly, e.g. rough/smooth, hard/soft, cold/warm. Work with battery circuits; why does bulb light? Shahrazad 'You put this here and this here (wire to each end of battery) the strings do it here to there (bulb to light battery). If you put this on top of the light (blue transparent plastic) and turn it on it's blue'. Using a motor 'This goes here and this goes there (wire to each end of battery) and it makes a noise. If I put paper on it, it goes round'.*

Under the teacher comment is written:

Shahrazad is going off to Algeria for the summer holidays. She may come back feeling shy and withdrawn as she did last year, but once she has begun to feel at home she will emerge. She is an affectionate child with an irrepressible laugh! Will miss her.

The parent comment dictated to the headteacher:

I am very happy with the report and the progress that the teachers have made on Shahrazad. I am grateful for the education she has had at James Lee.

The formative records at James Lee Nursery School from which these records of achievement are drawn, include records from the toddler's group in the school, giving interests, attitudes and relationships with parents/carer. On entry, an adapted 'All about Me' form is used. Staff target children and use a language and literacy form based on the Primary Language Record (PLR) and a physical development form together with the Keele Record traditionally used in the school to make up the child's profile. Daily meetings both in the morning and after school and a one-hour meeting each week, ensure that advanced planning is organic and caters for the individual child's needs. These are put on a grid-type chart daily showing what provision has to be made. When a child is four-years-old, parents are asked to help with the records, talking through their contribution with the headteacher a fortnight after guidance has been given on how to help. Samples of drawings, paintings and photographs are regularly put in the child's folder. All this information is sent to receiving schools.

The examples given demonstrate how individual schools, such as the James Lee Nursery School, are able to use the LEA or Record of Achievement in their own way. Since it is based on sound educational principles, it is an added resource for the school's record-keeping and encourages easy communication between schools. It also means that appropriate links can be made with the National Curriculum, or 5–14 Guidelines through the Programmes of Study. It is not sound practice to begin with the Attainment Targets, as that puts the cart before the horse.

BASELINE TESTING AND OTHER KINDS OF SUMMATIVE ASSESSMENT

Good record-keeping will automatically demonstrate on early meeting what the child *can* do. This is because it is about 'getting to know' the child. A specimen record kept on the first home-visit, or first week in the group, that can be coded for a particular focus is invaluable as baseline information. Other kinds of baseline 'tests' are probably going to operate in ways that cut across quality in early childhood education practice. Pre-packaged tests yield little information that can be positively acted upon. *Child Education* (August 1992), in its comments section, notes in relation to the second year of SATS (Standard Assessment Tests of seven-year-olds) in England and Wales:

> *... few felt that the SATS had shown them much about children that they did not know already. It seems unlikely the community will learn much from SATS results about the real achievements of individual schools. Research among parents shows that the terminology has proved confusing, and contrary to political opinion, they are not all that keen to see publication of League Tables comparing schools.*

In Scotland, where seventy-nine per cent of parents withdrew their children from SATS, when they were introduced, a new way forward has been found whereby teachers will decide at what point to test a child. This would be when the child was about to move from one level in reading, writing or mathematics to the next, irrespective of the time of year. In other words, pupils will take tests to confirm (or not) the teacher's understanding of their progress. The results would be shared with parents at meetings as part of the general report on progress. Schools will submit a summary of those tested to the School Board. Children with special educational needs will take part at the discretion of the headteacher in consultation with the parents. Local education authorities will send records of procedures and results for annual moderation by the Primary Assessment Unit. This approach is in keeping with the principles espoused in this book. It is to be hoped that it spreads south of the Border.

Records across the disciplines – Jean Stevens, health visitor

During a multi-professional diploma course in early childhood studies at Moray House College, Edinburgh, Jean Stevens learnt about Piagetian schemas. She wanted to add this as an additional tool to the conventional way of assessing general development and in partnership with parents, enhance the stimulation and quality of experience in the home environment. Here is an example (that she gives) of Linda, aged one year and three weeks:

> *Linda pulled herself to stand and pushed the cube under a cushion on the settee. She then crawled away. Linda laughs. Her mother says 'she does this type of thing quite a lot, maybe she copies her brother Jay'.*

Jean identifies this as an early enveloping schema. She also writes in her notes that:

> It transpired that at the end of the activity, Linda's mother mentioned her concern about Jay's behaviour who is four years and eight months old. It seems that every morning he has tied a skipping rope across his bedroom door much to the consternation of both his parents. The day before he had tied two teddy bears together with dressing gown cords for which he seemed to have a fascination.
>
> We were able to discuss the 'connecting schema' and Jay's mother was reassured that this was 'normal' behaviour in this context. She visibly relaxed and was reassured, keen to let his father know on his return from work. We discussed how to 'nourish' the schema using children's literature and activities.

On the second visit, one week later, envelopment is still evident in Linda's behaviour as it is in Jay's. Linda hides teddy in a tissue box and seeks out a handbag:

> Pulls to stand, then cruises along settee to attempt to explore adult's handbag. She spontaneously entered a new container of toys ... (p.39)
>
> Jay's connecting schema behaviour was exhibited in tied-up socks, socks with knots in them, and two large, pulling toys tied together. His parents were less ashamed of his behaviour and were considering what story books were available or what activity, to nourish this schema.

By the third visit his connecting schema was even viewed as 'inventive'. Jean writes:

> Linda was extending her enveloping schema to different objects and her parents were aware and happy to support this behaviour with appropriate language and environment, being much more aware as to what she was doing in making connections in her environment, and was not regarded as 'just naughty'.

Jean has reworked her regular development progress record to demonstrate her additional insight through schema. She adds:

> Schema may not emerge as a topic at each visit, but upon its spontaneous emergence or enquiry into the child's behaviour the concept can be shared with the parent.

FINAL THOUGHTS ON CURRENT PRACTICE

In this chapter we have looked at examples of current practice in record-keeping, soundly based on the principles of early childhood education. They involve parents, teamwork, observation of children, reflecting with a focus, leading to flexible advance planning.

Ideal characteristics of useful records – a tall order!

1   They keep faith with the heritage and basic principles of the early childhood traditions.
2   They help partnership with parents.
3   They encourage children to reflect on their own learning.
4   They need to be user-friendly, and make efficient, effective use of time and energy, so that they are easy to share with parents and colleagues in the team, across disciplines (e.g. health, social services, voluntary sector as well as education) and with the child's future teachers.
5   They might use a variety of techniques, written, audio and video tape recordings, photography, files of children's work, and records of achievement.
6   They link assessment of the child's progress with evaluation of what the child is offered.
7   They inform through sharing, planning and organisation, showing progress made and next steps.
8   They link with current requirements of the day, for example the Children Act or the National Curriculum as appropriate.
9   They need to be flexible and to grow organically.
10 They need to be capable of fine focus and to yield specific information.
11 They need to be easy to review and summarise.
12 They need to show starting points as well as growth points.

Perhaps this quotation from the Blockplay Research Group's publication *Exploring Learning: Young Children and Blockplay* (edited by Gura, 1992, directed by Tina Bruce) through which five groups of staff working in five very different educational settings regularly met and discussed record-keeping in relation to blockplay, best sums up the aspirations of this chapter.

Our experience has convinced us that our thinking was more rigorous and had greater depth and breadth because we were a group. We stuck at it because we were

*a group. We were getting somewhere in our thinking and practice because we were
a group. Colleagues who find themselves hoeing a lonely row might consider
forming a record-keeping collective. This could be within school (ideally the whole
school) or between schools.*

*Perhaps our most significant contribution to the record-keeping debate is the
glimpses offered of the potential of record-keeping as a shared point of entry for
adults and children in the gaining of insight to our own thought processes. As we
develop our capacity for self-conscious thought, record-keeping becomes less
formidable (p.152).*

This approach will help all those working with children under eight years of
age to put into appropriate perspective, the legal requirements of the National
Curriculum in England and Wales, or the 5–14 Guidelines in Scotland.

4 Getting To Know What We Want To Do

We All Need To Know What We Are Doing

Work at Redford House is under-pinned by a number of principles which are shared with the parents.

Children need to be active in their own learning as 'children have a natural appetite for movement' (Mollie Davies, 1969 p.73). She agrees with Susan Isaacs that children need to move just as they need to eat and sleep. In the long term …

> *children who constantly use their initiative to figure out wonderful things to do are more likely to learn deeply and go on to create new ideas than those who dutifully sit in front of the teacher, waiting for him or her to ask a question.*

(Kamii & Devries 1972–77)

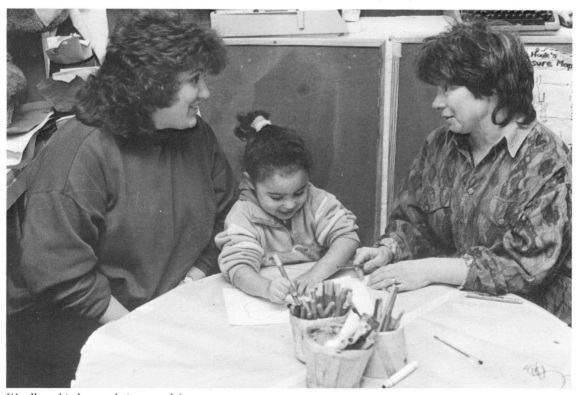

We all need to know what we are doing

Whatever the child's age, records are about children interacting with people and the whole environment. The starting point for staff at Redford House Nursery was to use what they already knew about record-keeping, and to value their strengths. Before reading on, it might be useful to re-read the introduction to Redford House at the beginning of the book.

During the review of record-keeping, it became apparent that each member of staff was familiar with the PIES format, which includes physical, intellectual, emotional and social aspects of the child's development and learning. Language (L) was added and emotional and social aspects were put together. Schemas were also added, making it PLIES. The observations recorded by staff and parents form the basis of curriculum planning. (See glossary for schemas). These are mainly on-the-spot observations but anecdotal observations are also added later to enhance and add to the information about a child.

The child development sheet devised by Joyce French (see Chapter 2) and the curriculum planning sheet shown opposite, enable staff to make appropriate provision which facilitates children's progress in different aspects of knowledge and understanding. Please look carefully now at the curriculum planning sheet opposite.

We can express the need to make appropriate provision simply by emphasising the need to observe, support and extend the child's learning. This is as true for a seven-year-old as it is for a three-year-old. Please look carefully now at the teacher observation sheet on page 72.

Observations, plus knowledge of child development including schemas, together with specially devised Focus sheets, make a useful base for record-keeping. The Focus sheets used at Redford House Nursery help staff to reflect on the observations they have made, in conjunction with the parents, and also help to plan the next step for the child's learning. Tricia David (1990 p.97) calls 'enmeshing evaluation of provision with assessment of the children' an important aspect of our work.

Staff observe the children, identify patterns in their development, and support and extend the children's emerging learning in educationally worthwhile ways. The framework of the schema is used as an added tool to the staff's knowledge of child development. Athey (1990 p.37) defines a schema as

a pattern of repeatable behaviour into which experiences are assimilated and that are gradually co-ordinated. Co-ordinations lead to higher-level and more powerful schemas.

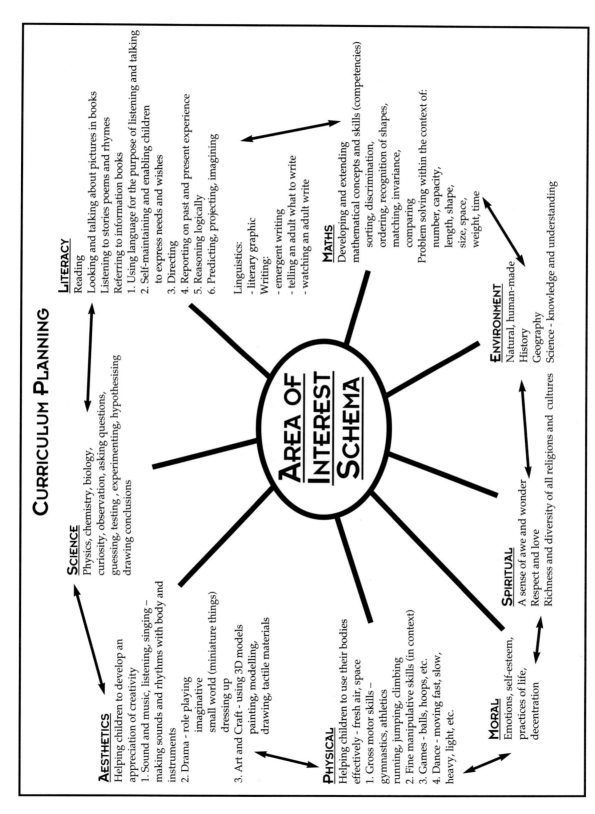

CURRICULUM PLANNING

AREA OF INTEREST SCHEMA

LITERACY
Reading
Looking and talking about pictures in books
Listening to stories poems and rhymes
Referring to information books
1. Using language for the purpose of listening and talking
2. Self-maintaining and enabling children to express needs and wishes
3. Directing
4. Reporting on past and present experience
5. Reasoning logically
6. Predicting, projecting, imagining

Linguistics:
- literary graphic
Writing:
- emergent writing
- telling an adult what to write
- watching an adult write

MATHS
Developing and extending mathematical concepts and skills (competencies)
sorting, discrimination, ordering, recognition of shapes, matching, invariance, comparing
Problem solving within the context of:
number, capacity, length, shape, size, space, weight, time

ENVIRONMENT
Natural, human-made
History
Geography
Science - knowledge and understanding

SPIRITUAL
A sense of awe and wonder
Respect and love
Richness and diversity of all religions and cultures

MORAL
Emotions, self-esteem, practices of life, decentration

PHYSICAL
Helping children to use their bodies effectively - fresh air, space
1. Gross motor skills – gymnastics, athletics running, jumping, climbing
2. Fine manipulative skills (in context)
3. Games - balls, hoops, etc.
4. Dance - moving fast, slow, heavy, light, etc.

AESTHETICS
Helping children to develop an appreciation of creativity
1. Sound and music, listening, singing – making sounds and rhythms with body and instruments
2. Drama - role playing imaginative small world (miniature things) dressing up
3. Art and Craft - using 3D models painting, modelling, drawing, tactile materials

SCIENCE
Physics, chemistry, biology, curiosity, observation, asking questions, guessing, testing , experimenting, hypothesising drawing conclusions

Table 6 Curriculum Planning (Joyce French)

Observe *schema connection*	Christopher (aged four) connecting train tracks, Lego, string, Sellotape, Constructo-straws, watertrays to baby baths using cardboard tubes and guttering. Whooshing fish, shells, stones, down the tubes. 'We've got a problem. The baby bath's getting too full.'
Support *language with* *action*	Make sure all the provision above is available for him to continue using it, with open access and staff showing sensitive interest. Share with parents.
Extend *through added* *provision carefully* *introduced and* *dialogue*	(a) Chinese water wheel (seen in *Guardian* 1992) made from bicycle wheel and yoghurt cups. Joined by children paying attention to rotation. Areas of knowledge: design, technology, history, geography. (b) Electric light bulbs, wires and batteries, to make circuits (science). (c) All under-pinned by language.

Teacher observation sheet to observe, support and extend Christopher's learning. Because these extensions were appropriate, Christopher and his friends concentrated for long periods of time

At Redford House Nursery, it has taken three years to integrate an understanding of schemas with traditional principles of good early years practice. Communication between parents and staff needs to be two-way so that each learns from the other. There needs to be some kind of shared focus.

Jo Weinberger, Peter Hannon and Cathy Nutbrown (1990) working with parents on language and literacy in Sheffield, have explored the fascination parents have for their own child's progress and development. Please look carefully now at the overview of record-keeping chart opposite.

PRE-VISIT AND ENTRY FORMS

Each family worker is responsible for collating observations on the children in their group and putting them in a folder. After much experimentation, staff have found the easiest way is for them is to use 'stick-it' notes, which can

OVERVIEW OF RECORD-KEEPING AT REDFORD HOUSE NURSERY	
Pre-entry/entry forms	(a) This is placed in child's file in the classroom with open access (see p.74) (b) This is placed in the office file to conform to the Children Act and is confidential
Parent observation sheet	This is filled in by parents at home, then put into the child's folder (see p.76)
Staff observations (on 'stick-it' notes)	These are kept by staff in the Nursery. The family worker collates the notes for the children in his/her group
Folder of regularly chosen samples of children's work with parent and staff observations	Drawings, paintings, photos, audio or video tape recordings, in home or nursery settings
Focus sheets - these are used to reflect on the observations that have been made. They are used to review and share progress with parents as far as practical constraints allow	P Physical development L Language and literacy I Intellectual (including maths and science E Emotional and social S Schemes—patterns of behaviour
Final report	For school transition

Overview of record-keeping at Redford House Nursery

quickly and easily be filed, along with examples of drawings, paintings, photographs or diagrams of children's three-dimensional or dance work. During a pre-visit or on entry, the family worker fills in the sheet shown on the next page (p.74), with the parent(s) and this goes at the front of each file. Another form, filled in with the family, complies with the Children Act and is kept separately.

REDFORD HOUSE NURSERY · ENTRY FORM

Name _____ Male/ Female _____

Date of birth _____ RTR / RI* Contracted hours _____

Position in family _____

Other family members and names _____

_____

Pets, if any, and names _____

First language of child _____

First language of parents _____

Language spoken at home _____

Does your child:

    Need to sleep during the day? _____

    Have a special toy or comforter? _____

    Have a special word for needing to go to the toilet? _____

    Deal with his/her own toilet needs? _____

    Have any particular fears or dislikes? _____

    Have any special needs (including diet) ? _____

_____

    Mostly use left or right hand? _____

What does your child particularly enjoy doing? _____

Is there anything you would like us to know? _____

Has your child any previous child care experience? _____

Family worker _____ Starting Date _____

*RTR–Richmond, Twickenham & Roehampton RI-Roehampton Institute   Leaving date _____

Redford House Nursery entry form

The parents are also introduced to the library and to a booklet about children's development and patterns in learning. This explains the approach used at Redford House. The booklet is loosely based on the *Rumpus* booklet (1986) produced by teachers, nursery nurses and parents in Cleveland. This gives opportunity for discussion in an informal atmosphere. In some settings, we recognise that translation of material into other languages will be an issue.

PARENT OBSERVATION SHEETS

The parents are invited to fill in at home, observation sheets, (like the one shown on the next page (p.76) which emphasises observing the child during spontaneous play. Discovering patterns in their child's learning and development, is something many parents find exciting, stimulating and rewarding. Others, often because of pressures in their lives, find it harder and staff try to find extra time to talk more with parents in these situations. These parent observation sheets, when returned, also go into the child's folder, along with the 'stick-it' notes, dated examples of the child's work and photographs of the child 'in action' or of models and constructions. Folders are kept in boxes where the parents can have open access to them. Any confidential information is kept elsewhere.

STAFF OBSERVATION, USING 'STICK-IT' LABELS

Staff observe the child's interaction with peers and adults. They also observe spontaneous representations, either two-dimensional in paintings and drawings or three-dimensional in block play, woodwork, collage, recycled materials, home corner and small world, Lego or other construction toys. In fact, whatever children are using or doing is noted. Because it is not the policy to provide prescriptive, didactic activities for the children, such as cutting out a sheep shape and expecting the children to cover it with cotton wool, staff are able to record the progression of the child's own ideas, thinking and understanding. In short, the aim is to record the child's learning. Staff are concerned to encourage learning across specific areas of knowledge in the curriculum such as mathematics, science, dance, language and literacy and technology (see curriculum planning sheet p.71). Being clear about areas of knowledge helps early childhood workers to be articulate about the child's learning.

PARENT OBSERVATION SHEET
(observe, support, extend)

Name	Time & date

Parent observation sheet (observe, support, extend) from Redford House Nursery

USING THE ENTRY FORM: PARENT OBSERVATION SHEET AND STAFF OBSERVATIONS

In the following section, we shall see how the different forms interrelate, giving a whole picture of William and Alice, two children attending the nursery.

It is however, important to remember that the examples of William and Alice given in this chapter can only be very tiny vignettes when compared with all the formative, continuous records made on the parent and staff observation sheets. A book like this can only show a glimpse of a child's development and learning.

Getting to know William during his first week in January – using the entry form

The Redford House entry form shows that William is just three years old, and has started at Redford House soon after a hernia operation. He is English-speaking but speech is unclear. Sometimes he sleeps during the day at home. He lives with his mother, father and older sister (aged seven). He attended a day nursery from babyhood. He sometimes brings in a special toy which changes regularly, for example one day a bat, another it might be a ball. He is fairly independent with eating and toilet needs. He is afraid of monsters. At home he particularly enjoys books, puzzles, cuddles and physical activities. He has grommets in his ears, and he is left-handed. (See the parent observation sheet on the next page (p.78).)

We can see his mother finding quicker and quicker ways to record, developing her own symbols to do so. His mother told the family worker she keeps an observation sheet both in the kitchen and the bedroom.

Staff observations of William

These observations were made on 'stick-it' labels in on-the-spot situations and inserted in the file regularly.

1   7 January beige room. Parted from mother without any distress. Pushed shopping trolley. Put blocks inside. Moved blocks into house. Tipped out on to table.
2   8 January outside – digging in earth. Carrying earth on spade making pile in playground back and forth.

PARENT OBSERVATION SHEET - WILLIAM		
William	Time	Date of observation
Moved twenty balloons from his and sister's room to front bedroom		6.1
Threw all the balloons downstairs one or two at a time - peals of laughter	a.m.	7.1
Noticed scribbles on wall - bedroom ≡ (15 inches long) and on the staircase - one long line the whole length		
Put toy cups into basket and carried around house. "lunchbox"	8a.m.	16.1
Cars arranged in a semi-circle ⁓ııı⁓ "traffic-jam"	1.00pm	12.1
Pile of plates from toy kitchen to floor, walked on them as stepping stones	6.15pm	28.1

Parent observation sheet for William (original version) from Redford House Nursery

3   9 January beige room. Transported items from house to block area. Dumped everything in a pile in the corner. Pushing trolley around the room.

4   10 January red room. Filling bottles with water. Putting full bottles in shopping trolley and empty cardboard box. Spent forty-five minutes at water tray.

5   13 January outside. Climbing up and down on apparatus. Backward and forward movement. Moving in straight lines fast and slow.

6   14 January outside. Piece of string was attached to the wooden trike. William held the string pulling the trike from one side of the playground to the other. Repeated action.

7   15 January outside. Running and pushing the pram around the playground up and down the slope backwards and forwards.

8   16 January outside. Holding the spade in his left hand. William dug deep into the earth. With earth piled high on the spade he walked to the top of the slope.

9   21 January red room. Filling bottles. Tipping water out. Filling up again. Walked over to junk basket. Chose a box. Filled it with water. Banged two hands together splattering water inside collapsing box. Shrieks of laughter. Low threshold crying. Unable to negotiate under any circumstances. Sitting on adult's lap, listening to story, sucking thumb, holding ear. Needs lots of cuddles – unwell.

10 22 January beige room. Moving blocks from block area to house knocking things down en route. Going back and forth. Placing blocks across front of house – 'you can't come in' arranging blocks in straight line.

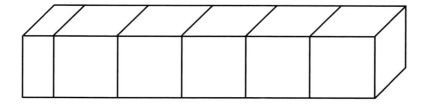

Not all the examples of William during this period are included from either parent or staff observation sheets because there are far too many. Those chosen are typical of his activity during this period. At this stage staff were not yet using Focus sheets, and so tended to evaluate in their own way at the end of the first week in the nursery. Here follows the week one evaluation.

Initial impression of William on entering nursery

William appears physically small in stature, full of energy, interested in everything.

Observations made here and at home show that he likes to contain and transport and when he has initiated the task he is able to concentrate for long periods of time.

Negotiating with William may be necessary to provide him with alternatives or choices which will enable his needs to be met positively.

His language indicates some delay. Through lack of hearing his pronunciation and speech is not always clear. I feel his lack of communicating skills is sometimes reflected in his ability to negotiate with his peers.

William likes to lead. He plays alone, alongside others and with Max on a one to one basis. Within a small group he is experiencing the need to take turns and to understand the needs of others. He enjoys looking at books and stories: sitting on an adult's lap listening to a story as well as in a large or small group.

FOCUS SHEETS

After experimentation with several cumbersome systems which were anything but user friendly, Focus sheets were developed and have replaced these regular evaluations as a way of reviewing progress. This allows staff to focus observations (in particular directions) after they are made, for example looking at the child's relationships, mathematics, physical coordination and so on. The Focus sheets are based on PLIES. These serve as *aides mémoire* or prompts which help staff and parents to reflect on their observations. One or two observations can be used with different Focus sheets. Focus sheets could also be developed by those working with older children (five to eight years) which would cover the programmes of study in the National Curriculum, and yet remain true to the principles of early-childhood education. As we saw with Christopher (aged four) on p.72, in the work he did on electric bulbs, wires and batteries to make circuits, he was already mastering aspects of the Science Programme.

Using The Focus Sheets

This section shows how the Focus sheets on William were used at regular intervals to reflect on his progress and future needs in emotional and social areas, and in mathematics and science. It is important to look first at the parent and staff observations, and then at the Focus sheet, and not the other way round. Later in the chapter, Focus sheets are used to reflect on Alice's future needs in relation to physical development, language and literacy. The Focus sheets relating to schemas are used for both children. This means that examples are given of all the Focus sheets making up PLIES. It cannot be over emphasised that a Focus sheet is not a check-list, but an aid to reflection on specimen record observations after they have been made. It is not necessary to consider everything on the Focus sheet at any one time. It may be necessary to add to it on occasions if there seem to be gaps. It is used together with the parent and staff observation sheets, to focus discussion and plan the next step in the child's learning.

We have chosen to introduce the emotional and social Focus sheet first in this section, because it is a major concern amongst staff that they do not write seemingly negative things about any child. Socially unacceptable behaviour was at first shared verbally between parents and staff. This was in order to work out strategies and achieve a consistently constructive approach. The emotional and social Focus sheet has arisen as a positive way of dealing with these difficult areas. The form shown on the next page (p.82) was used to extract relevant information from the staff and parent observations and to review William's progress using written records.

Using this Focus sheet we can see that William is fairly independent in dealing with his basic needs. He needs some help wiping his bottom after the toilet, and needs reminding to wash his hands. He needs some help with dressing such as with his socks and shoes. He has difficulty with turn taking and sharing. He indulges in hitting and pushing and is possessive of objects and space. He is affectionate towards adults. He has a strong sense of humour. He is involved in solitary play except with adults.

Staff observation – using 'stick-it' labels – in February
William 21 February beige room. William taking blocks off trolley. Putting into bag. Bag into shopping trolley. Walked away from block area. Max at block area playing with blocks. W returns jumping up and down, shouting. Max continues to play – W bit him.

Emotional and social development Focus sheet used for William in February
The prompts on the Focus sheet most useful here are his strategies to gain what is needed. He is biting and shouting. He remains possessive of objects and space. He is however, more aware of other children, but although not always solitary now, still needs adult support in developing access strategies for playing with other children.

EMOTIONAL AND SOCIAL DEVELOPMENT FOCUS SHEET - REDFORD HOUSE NURSERY		
Eating meals, dressing/undressing, toilet, washing and brushing teeth	Uses cutlery, spills, talks to neighbours, level of dependence/help, day/night	Independence, basic needs
Decentration	Aware of other children understanding danger, role play, comforting other children, helpfulness, turn taking, sharing	
Pushing, tantrums, biting, spitting, scratching, hitting, whinging, crying, shouting, swearing, sulking, bribing, bullying		Strategies to gain what is needed socially
Affection Friendships	- Children - Adults - Pets	
Humour		
Joining play Balance of play	Access strategies: - circling - side-by-side - gives up easily Watching others play, needs adult or older child, solitary, parallel, co-operative	

Emotional and social development Focus sheet – Redford House Nursery (based on (Mary Sheridan 1973))

Mother observation (February)
4/5 large hankie on stick of wood – waved in air looking at reflection in mirror. 'It's like the wind.'

Looking at the mathematics and science Focus sheet on the next page (p.84) and taking the staff and parent observations from January and February, we can see that William is exploring space, and in particular volume and capacity of blocks, earth, water in containers. He is interested in the sameness of blocks, different length lines (blocks, string etc.). He is establishing invariance that one shovelful of earth is the same wherever it is placed in the playground. He is making a one-to-one correspondence from the reflection of the hankie on the stick of wood. He is learning about the properties of matter, for example that earth, wooden blocks, and wet cardboard differ in the way they behave. The hankie-waving is likened to the force of the wind, as is pulling the trike along with the string.

Before reading on, please turn to the Schema focus sheets shown overleaf on pp.85 and 86.

Transporting
Taking balloons from one room to another
Take earth from one pile to another
Carrying picnic basket from one place to another
Pushing shopping trolley with blocks in it
Filling bottles with water and transferring them, and then tipping them out
Transporting blocks using bags and trolley

Trajectories
Hitting, biting, throwing
Riding a trike in straight lines
Line of plates on the floor
Making lines with string
Digging in earth
Moving in straight lines with varied speeds
Arranging blocks in straight line
Noticing striped scribble on the wall
Waving a stick covered in a hankie

MATHEMATICS		
Matching	One-to-one correspondence e.g. cup and saucer cardinal numbers 1, 2, 3, objects etc.	
Space	Near/far over/under behind/infront of high/low volume capacity	
Sorting	Naming common properties Classifying	(is/is not) red wellies/not red wellies whole biscuit/not whole biscuit
Making comparisons	Likeness Differences Longer/shorter (comparisons)	eg. rabbit bigger than hamster faster/slower
Ordering	Ordinal numbers Cardinal numbers	1st, 2nd, 3rd morning routine, recipe, seasons turn taking
Invariance	Permanent identity of an object	e.g. Jack in the box, sand, water, clay etc.
Recognising shapes	Solid shapes - cubes, spheres etc. 2-dimensional - triangles etc.	recycled materials furniture, books

SCIENCE	
Natural World Animals, insects, birds, amphibians and fish etc. Where they live (habitat) What they eat How they eat (claws, jaws, beak, feet etc.) How do they protect themselves (camouflage, claws, tusks, fur for warmth, oil on ducks, waterproof, shell etc.) Plants, trees, flowers Food chains Leaves, tree trunks, scent, colours on flowers, seed dispersal	**Properties of matter** Sand, water, clay, wood, paint Weaving, rug making **Transformations** Reversible - sugar/salt in water Irreversible - boil an egg cut down a tree Mixtures Forces - levers, pulleys Gravity - parachutes Light - torches, lanterns, candles Sound - home-made instruments Heat - cookery, fire Electricity - circuits Floating and sinking Simple technology Reflection

Mathematics and Science Focus sheet based on chart devised by Rosemary Roberts, Oxfordshire

Schema Focus sheet taken from 'RUMPUS' (see glossary & bibliography)

Transporting

A child may move objects or collections of objects from one place to another, perhaps using a bag, pram or truck.

Positioning

A child may be interested in placing objects in particular positions e.g. on top of something, around the edge, behind. Paintings and drawings also often show evidence of this.

Orientation

This schema is shown by interest in a different viewpoint as when a child hangs upside down or turns objects upside down.

Dab

A graphic schema used in paintings randomly or systematically to form patterns or to represent, for example, eyes, flowers, buttons etc.

Dynamic Vertical (and horizontal)

A child may show evidence of particular interest by actions such as climbing, stepping-up and down or lying flat. These schemas may also be seen in constructions, collages or graphically. After schemas of horizontality and verticality have been explored separately the two are often used in conjunction to form crosses or grids. These are very often systematically explored on paper and interest is shown in everyday objects such as a cooling tray, grills, nets etc.

Trajectory

A fascination with things moving or flying through the air e.g. balls, aeroplanes, rockets, catapults, frisbees - and indeed, anything that can be thrown. When expressed through child's own body movements, this often becomes large arm and leg movements, kicking, punching etc.

Diagonality

Usually later than the previous schemas this one emerges via the construction of ramps, slides and sloping walls. Drawings begin to contain diagonal lines forming roofs, hands, triangles, zig-zags.

Enclosure

A child may build enclosures with blocks, Lego, large crates etc. perhaps naming them boats, ponds, beds. The enclosure is sometimes left empty, sometimes carefully filled in. An enclosing line often surrounds paintings and drawings while a child is exploring this schema.

Enveloping

This is often an extension of enclosure. Objects, space or the child herself are completely covered. She may wrap things in paper, enclose them in pots or boxes with covers or lids, wrap herself in a blanket or creep under a rug. Paintings are sometimes covered over with a wash of colour or scrap collages glued over with layers of paper or fabric.

Schema Focus sheet taken from 'RUMPUS' (Cleveland LEA)

'RUMPUS' (CONTINUED)

CIRCLES
Circles appear in drawings and paintings as heads, bodies, eyes, ears, hands, feet etc. They are also used in representing animals, flowers, wheels, the sun and a wide variety of other things.

SEMI-CIRCULARITY
Semi-circles are also used graphically as features, parts of bodies and other objects. Smiles, eyebrows, ears, rainbows and umbrellas are a few of the representational uses for this schema as well as parts of letters of the alphabet.

RADIAL
Again common in paintings and drawings. Spiders, suns, fingers, eyelashes, hair often appear as a series of radials.

ROTATION
A child may become absorbed by things which turn e.g. taps, wheels, cogs and keys. She may roll cylinders along, or roll herself. She may rotate her arms, or construct objects with rotating parts in wood or scrap materials.

CONNECTION
Scrap materials may be glued, sewn and fastened into lines; pieces of wood are nailed into long connecting constructions. Strings, rope, wool etc. are used to tie objects together, often in complex ways. Drawings and paintings sometimes show a series of linked parts. The opposite of this schema may be seen in separation where interest is shown in disconnecting assembled or attached parts.

ORDERING
A child may produce paintings and drawings with ordered lines or dabs; collages or constructions with items of scrap carefully glued in sequence. She may place blocks, vehicles or animals in lines and begin to show interest in 'largest' and 'smallest'.

TRANSFORMING
A child may become interested in materials which change shape, colour, consistency etc. e.g. ice melting, potatoes cooking, clay hardening, paint mixing.

ONE TO ONE CORRESPONDENCE
There is often evidence of this schema in scrap collages and constructions where a child say, for example, glues a button inside each bottle top or places a piece of paper inside each cup of an egg box.

FUNCTIONAL DEPENDENCY
Although causal relationships are not fully appreciated, interest may be seen in the dependency of one function upon another. For example, a child may draw a lift with a button beside it and say, 'You have to press this for the lift to come' or pretend to turn an ignition key 'so that the engine will start'.

Schema Focus Sheet taken from 'RUMPUS' (continued)

Using observations to support and extend William's learning across the curriculum in order to offer him what he needs

Although this section is looking at William's needs in particular, records of other children indicate that they will also benefit from some of this provision.

The Focus sheets have alerted us to what William is doing, based on observations. In this section we look at curriculum planning (what we need to offer William) using PLIES.

Looking at the curriculum planning sheet (see p.90) we can begin to extend William's learning in all areas of the curriculum. We need to remember, as the *Starting with Quality* Report (DES, 1990) states, that all areas of knowledge are linked and cannot be separated out.

William is supported in pursuing his persistent concerns providing that they are not unsafe or socially unacceptable. Nicholls (1986 p.20) quoting Athey says

> to recognise a schema is not necessarily to embrace it, and some schemas in action
> 'may not be acceptable to adults' but even where this is so, it is reassuring to both
> parents and staff to realise that the basis for some inconvenient behaviour is
> learning rather than naughtiness.

Records help us to provide constructive alternatives to challenging behaviour

It is not acceptable for William to bite. He has begun to use a different type of trajectory as well as biting, which is hitting. This could be more easily extended from hitting people (unacceptable) to hitting plastic bottles strung on a washing

Supporting learning – a pulley

line outside, using bats and balls. Extending in this way helps him to learn, with practice, about hand/eye coordination; about forces in physics and estimation of distance in mathematical space.

William's mother has indicated how helpful it has been to develop some strategies which are constructive in dealing with some of his extremely challenging behaviour. It is noticeable that when children are satisfied, their need to pursue these actions in aggressive ways decreases. Being given what you need helps you to learn in ways which are socially acceptable.

The curriculum planning chart on the next page (p.90) shows how William, and other children with similar needs, are helped to learn.

Getting to know Alice during her first week, August – using the entry form

The entry form shows that Alice is nearly three years old, has had two nannies and attended a workplace nursery for one year. Her first language is English. She occasionally sleeps for twenty minutes, often after weekends. She has a special blanket at home but does not choose to bring it to the nursery. She holds herself if she needs to go to the toilet and may need reminding. She has a tendency towards asthma and has a stutter, particularly with 'W' and 'N'. She is right-handed. She enjoys gluing, sticking, cutting, felt-tips, drawing, play dough, slides/climbing, reading. Please look overleaf at the Parent Observation Sheet and Alice's drawing, (pp.91 and 92).

Staff observations of Alice

1   25/8 does cutting. Uses stapler. Finger paints. Plays in water. Outside – plays on bike, tractor. Sits on wooden horse. Plays on slide.

2   26/8 spend most of day in beige room/on mountain (see the photograph on p.93), in sand, in home corner. Slept for almost three-quarters of an hour, reluctant to wake up. Nose blocked up.

3   27/8 cries when mother leaves but stops immediately she has gone. Sits on C's lap. Uses scissors proficiently (right hand) to cut out pictures on cards. Gets down after about ten minutes. Sticks Sellotape on paper. Has breakfast. Paints on paper on table. Folds paper over, says 'look' to me, smiling. Blows bubbles (using bubbling pipes).

4   28/8 comes in 8.50 a.m. A few momentary tears. Asks to join other children digging up potatoes. Clings on to plastic bag of cereal brought from home. Holds spade shifting it round in soil. Goes to play on slide. Comes inside. Lets go of bag. Sits at tables and prints with paint selecting shapes with handles pushing down on paper. Does two pictures folding paper over in second one. Is reluctant to share shapes with Tom but does so with negotiation with adult. Sits outside on bench eating cereal out of bag

CURRICULUM PLANNING CHART

WILLIAM'S TRANSPORTING & TRAJECTORY SCHEMA JAN/FEB

SCIENCE
SPLASH PAINTING (see mathematics) A PULLEY over the sand tray, using William's trajectory schema, helps him to encounter light/heavy, and forces in physics.

LITERACY
The POST OFFICE satisfies William in that he can stamp the letters and deliver them. Stories offered include *The Hungry Giant* (about a giant who hits) *Mr Gumpy's Outing* and poetry *Noisy poems*.
Whilst involved in these experiences, genuine conversations take place around things which are of great interest to him.
His language has developed dramatically. This is a combination of improved hearing since the adjustment of his grommets and being supported and extended through dialogue with adults whilst involved in activities which fascinate him.

MATHEMATICS
SPLASH PAINTING involves mathematics and distance. Post Office play with different sized bags and baskets and all the problems associated with getting big boxes into small containers before being able to transport them, offer different experiences (volume, capacity, problem-solving).

PHYSICAL
Everything William does indoors and outdoors offers him opportunities for gross and fine motor co-ordinations. Grommets in his ears help him to experience fully the physical environment.

ENVIRONMENT
Gardening and digging ready for vegetable planting and in particular for William to transport earth to fill garden tubs.

AESTHETICS/TECHNOLOGY
PRINTING and WOODWORK help William to hit and stab in acceptable ways, without putting him under pressure to co-operate with others before he is ready to do so. His CONSTRUCTIONS with BLOCKS, or rockets using Sellotape and RECYCLED MATERIALS, (up and down, side to side trajectories) were praised and valued by adults, which contributed to his positive self-esteem.

MORAL
Using pulleys he began to turn-take. (See also constructions and printing and woodwork.)

SPIRITUAL
Gardening (free environment) encourages a sense of awe and wonder. Having his constructions valued leads to respect and love. Collaborating with others helps him appreciate other cultures and diversity amongst human beings.

Curriculum Planning Chart for William using PLIES

PARENT OBSERVATION SHEET DURING THE EARLY DAYS - ALICE. AUG		
Alice	Time	Date of observation
Drawing a cricket pitch with all of Daddy's friends in it. Then cutting patches out. (straight lines)	0900	22.8
Drawing circles drew "M" "for monkey"	18.00	22.8
At a party singling out one friend and then going up and down slide doing counting.		Mon. 24.8
Playing in garden with the earth making a pile then sweeping it all over patio!	17.35	Tues 25.8
Building a tower with duplo. Making a church with a steeple. Colouring a picture and keeping within lines.	17.35	Wed 26.8
Playing with P. Pat, jigsaw and soldier. Turning it over and putting the pieces on the wood side. Playing on climbing frame and slide.	18.30	Thurs 27.8
Building a rocket with all the duplo. Playing with it for the first time in years. Asking for the same story to be read learning it inside out.	17.00	Sat 29.8

Parent observation sheet for Alice – her first week at nursery

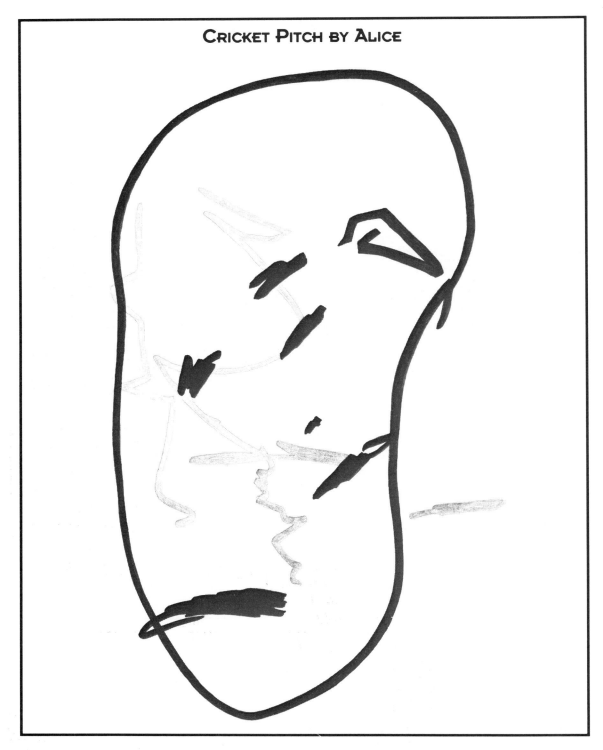

CRICKET PITCH BY ALICE

My Daddy playing cricket with his friends *by Alice*

The mountain

observing children. Says to C 'Who is that little girl?' pointing to child who has not been to nursery before. Afternoon – outside on slide, climbing up ladder, jumping from top of frame. Inside – plays with clay and water alongside group of children. 'Squidgying' it around in her hands. Sits and puts wooden balls on wooden helter-skelter with three respective children. Some communication between them. Claire later joins her and Alice tells C when it's her turn, waiting accordingly. A moves to woodwork bench and spends considerable time sawing through pieces of wood. Mother arrives and sits with her. After a while she moves to a table of Duplo and mother sits alongside her.

Summary of Alice's first week

At this stage Alice's family worker was still doing the end of the first week evaluation. This is what she wrote:

Alice has coped well in her new environment. She has interacted well with adults and has communicated her needs to them. She has shown determination and independence.

Alice has mostly participated in parallel play. She has at times interacted with other children on a one-to-one level. She has observed the other children, quickly remembering their names and enquiring after those she does not know.

LB has spoken to mother about intermittent hearing loss. Her speech has been unclear at times. She has an apparent stutter. She has suffered from a blocked nose.

Alice has paid particular attention to gross motor activities, for example the slide, the mountain, the bike, gaining in confidence as the week has progressed. She has enjoyed cutting with scissors and sawing at the woodwork bench. Alice has enjoyed immersing her hands in paint and clay, (query trajectory/query enveloping).

As yet there are only a few observations about Alice, since she has only been at Redford House Nursery for one month. However the observations during that time are sufficient to enable staff to use Focus sheets in assessing her progress to date, and in advance planning for her needs. The first Focus sheet opposite relates to her physical development, and the second (p.96) relates to her language and literacy development. The schema Focus sheet is also used.

Physical development Focus sheet – Alice – August

Alice enjoys climbing, jumping from heights, digging, sliding, tricycles and steering. Painting and drawing demonstrate pincergrasp, pencil control and attention to detail. She builds Duplo constructions and uses scissors competently.

She is mouth breathing because of her blocked nose, and this produces nasal articulation. However she has normal syntax, for example 'Who is that little girl?' Her entry form highlights her stutter. The staff suspected an intermittent hearing loss. The family GP had seen Alice when her nose was not blocked. Her mother decided to seek further advice after discussion with LB and is pursuing the matter, arranging a visit to an ENT specialist. This highlights the importance of an early development in partnership between parents and professionals.

Language and literacy Focus sheet – Alice – August

Alice expresses simple needs, asking to join other children. She asks questions, using simple sentences. 'Who is that little girl?'
She talks both one-to-one and in a small group, for example helter-skelter observation.
She describes her drawing (the cricket pitch on page 92).
She writes the letter M. An anecdotal observation, (written after it happened) shows that she recognises A. She asks for the same story to be read, learning it

PHYSICAL FOCUS SHEET REDFORD HOUSE NURSERY

LARGE MOVEMENTS

Orientating Body	**Body in relation to objects**
Running	Steering
Walking	Pushing
Climbing	Pulling
Jumping	Riding - Tricycles
Hopping	Bicycling
Skipping	Scooting
Somersaults	Throwing
Tiptoe	Catching
Cross-legged	Kicking
Sitting	Bouncing
Sliding	Stairs
Swinging	
Digging	
Stunts	
Rolling	

FINE MOVEMENTS & VISION	HEARING & SPEECH
Pincer grasp	Articulation
Pencil grasp	Speech flow (one-word sentence, two-word sentence etc.)
Builds towers	Loudness of voice
(Note other constructions)	Range of pitch
Preferred hand use	Use of past, present and future tense
Looks at details in picture books	Mouth breathing
Drawings -	
note marks for co-ordination	
Scissor use	

Physical Focus sheet – Redford House Nursery (based on Mary Sheridan 1973)

LANGUAGE & LITERACY FOCUS SHEET	
SPEAKING & LISTENING	**READING & STORYING**

Talks readily at home/nursery staff
Talks about what she has done and past
    experience
Talks about what she is doing
Describes things
Plans ahead
Uses simple sentences
Expresses simple needs
Talks one to one, small/large group
Follows simple instructions
Listens attentively one to one
Initiates conversation
Asks questions e.g. how, what, when,
    where and why
	Interest in books
	Enjoys songs/rhymes/poems
	Enjoys stories read/told
	Joins in rhymes/songs
	Favourite stories
	Looks at books alone
	Retells familiar stories
	Sings spontaneously
	'Reads' back own writing
	'Reads' from left to right
	Makes up stories
	Recognises letters from print
	Recognises print conveys meaning
	Knows where a book begins
	Devises props e.g. puppets

WRITING	

Enjoys using pencils and crayons
Makes marks as writing
Can draw recognisable shape/object
Shows interest in writing e.g. lists, signs, logos and brand names
Writes own name using marks
Writes some letters
Writes own name using letters
Writes name (conventional letters)
'Writes' own stories using -   marks
                          letters and marks
                          conventional letters

Enjoys writing spontaneously
Makes own books with pictures -
                          likes to copy words
                          needs a scribe
                          makes own writing

Language and literacy Focus sheet from Redford House Nursery

inside out. She sings spontaneously. Anecdotal records also show that she is willing to make marks on paper to represent her name.

Schema Focus sheet – Alice – August

Enveloping

- Finger painting, covering her hands, folding paper over, digging up potatoes, plastic bag of cereal, covering picture in a jigsaw

- Drawing an enclosure with things inside

- Making piles/heaps and covering the patio

- Bubbles

Trajectories

- Cutting straight lines, building a Duplo tower, sweeping, church with a tall steeple, rocket

- Bike, tractor, stapler

- Bubbles, digging, sawing, climbing, jumping, using slide.

Observe, support and extend Alice's learning

Because Alice is so new to the nursery environment, she is still exploring what is there. This means that staff do not yet need to concentrate on making specific provision for her, as there are still many new experiences for her which are appropriately supporting her existing knowledge and extending her in many different ways.

Joan Tamburrini (1981) emphasises the importance of an extending style of working with young children, alongside supporting strategies. At Redford House Nursery the weekly plan is used flexibly and is introduced as and when it is appropriate, in response to the children's needs. This is in the spirit of Lilli Nielsson's statement (1984 p.17)

> *What the child is offered is based upon what the child at each time needs for his or her further development. The questions about what he or she in fact needs just now could be solved by a very detailed assessment about what he or she is in fact able to do, and a discussion about which sort of surroundings he or she needs to use this ability to go through the next step of development.*

FINAL REVIEW

When children move to the primary school, a final review is made. A report is written and the child's folder, containing observations and examples of work, goes to the parent. The parent can then share these records with the staff of the receiving school.

Charlie's final review – transition to school at four years nine months

Although staff at Redford House Nursery use schemas as an additional tool to observation, support and extension of development and learning, few of the receiving schools are knowledgeable about this way of working with children. This is of no consequence, because schemas only serve to enhance traditional approaches to development and learning with which early years teachers are familiar. It is not necessary therefore, to mention schemas as such in writing a child's final report.

Charlie has been at Redford House for eighteen months attending on a flexible basis. Charlie relates well to adults and mixes cooperatively with large and small groups of children, and is a very able negotiator.

Charlie is extremely good at solving problems and coming up with creative solutions and is able to think logically about what he is doing. He loves stories, is able to re-tell them and make up his own. He recognises some words and letters. He has a good understanding of number and spatial concepts. Although his speech is not always clear, he uses language well and has a wide vocabulary.

He has produced some lovely spontaneous creative models including recently one of our incubator. He is a competent drawer and can write his name alone, and is beginning to do other writing. He has shown a great interest in map-making and maps which we have used on our walks around the grounds. Charlie is confident in his use of large climbing apparatus and is well coordinated generally.

FINALLY

The staff at Redford House do not see the present record-keeping system as written in tablets of stone: record-keeping, like any other aspect of curriculum development, is part of a continuous process.

CONCLUSION

According to Gail McCail (1991 p.4) in the Moray House/BAECE pre-five environment quality survey made of record-keeping, we should be aiming for the following:

> *Records are kept for each child who is a consistent user, comprising emergency, health and family information. Such records are open to the parents concerned and to professionals involved with the child but are otherwise closed. Profiles are also kept, (regularly updated by observation in the facility) which record the child's progress on a broad front – interpersonal, physical, linguistic, cognitive. These are passed on with the child to infant school.*
>
> *Also, parents are regularly consulted about their children's records and regularly contribute to them. A network of appropriate contacts has been built up from whom relevant information is regularly received (e.g. health visitor, GP, social worker).*

Redford House Nursery, together with all the examples mentioned in this book, meets these criteria. However, current staffing levels in most early years settings rarely give staff non-contact time in which to write records.

Professor Chris Pascal is developing an evaluation schedule to assess what is meant by 'quality in educational provision for young children'. She is using ten dimensions:

- aims and objectives

- curriculum

- teaming and teaching strategies

- assessment

- planning and record-keeping

- staffing

- physical involvement, relationships and interactions

- equal opportunities

- parental partnership and liaison

- monitoring and evaluation

The project is a collaborative one, including early-childhood educators, parents and children. The study, when published, will help us to monitor and record quality in what we offer children.

We end by repeating the ideal characteristics of useful records which apply across disciplines in education, care, health and the voluntary sector for all children, at least until the age of eight, including those children legally required to follow the National Curriculum or the 5–14 Guidelines in Scotland.

1   They keep faith with the heritage and basic principles of the early childhood traditions.
2   They help partnership with parents.
3   Children are encouraged to reflect on their own learning.
4   They need to be user-friendly and make efficient, effective use of time and energy, so that they are easy to share with parents, and colleagues in the team, across disciplines, (e.g. health, social services, voluntary sectors as well as education) and with the child's future teachers.
5   They might use a variety of techniques such as written, audio and visual tape recording, photography, files of children's work and records of achievement.
6   They link assessment of the child with evaluation of what the child is offered.
7   The records inform through sharing, planning and organisation, showing progress made and next steps.
8   They link with current requirements of the day, for example the Children Act or the National Curriculum as appropriate.
9   They need to be flexible and to grow organically.
10 They need to be capable of fine focus and to yield specific information.
11 They need to be easy to review and summarise.
12 They need to show starting points, as well as growth points.

Records are about getting to know the child, and what the child needs.

BIBLIOGRAPHY

Almy, M., (1975) *The Early Childhood Educator at Work*. New York: McGraw Hill.

Athey, C., (1990) *Extending Thought in Young Children: A Parent–Teacher Partnership*. London: Paul Chapman Publishing Ltd.

Axeline, V., (1964) *Dibs – In Search of Self*. Boston: Houghton–Mifflin.

Barnet LEA, (May, 1990) *Barnet Nursery Record*.

Barnet LEA, (1992) *Barnet, Entry Filing: A Framework for Developing a Policy*.

Barrs, M.; Ellis, S.; Hester, H. and Thomas, A., (1989: Reprinted) *Primary Language Record. Handbook for Teachers*. ILEA/CLPE.

Barrs, M.; Ellis, S.; Hester, H. and Thomas, A., (1990) *The Primary Language Record and the National Curriculum*. London: CLPE.

Bartholomew, L.H., (1985) It's all very well in theory, but what about in practice? Some ideas on innovation. *Early Child Development and Care*, 19, No. 3: 237–50.

Bartholomew, L., (1989) Investigative play. *Child Education*, 66, No. 5: 30–2.

Bates, S., (November 17, 1992) A chorus of disapproval. *Education Guardian*.

Bennett, N. and Kell, J., (1989) *A Good Start? Four Year Olds in Infant Schools*. Oxford: Basil Blackwell.

Bissex, G., (1980) Gyns at Wrk. Massachusetts and England: Harvard University Press.

Bowlby, J., (1971) Volume 1. *Attachment and Loss*. Harmondsworth, Middlesex: Penguin Books Ltd.

Bradford LEA, (1991) *A set of articles on Schema*. Compiled by Sheila Rye, advisory teacher.

Bradford LEA, (1992) *Assessing Children at the Start of School*.

Bruce, T., (1985) It's all very well in practice, but what about in theory? *Early Child Development and Care*, 19, No. 3: 151–73.

Bruce, T., (1987) *Early Childhood Education*. Sevenoaks: Hodder and Stoughton.

Bruce, T., (1988) The Implications of the National Curriculum for Early Childhood Education. *TACTYC Journal*, 9, No. 1, (Autumn): 1–22.

Bruce, T., (1989a) Parents as Partners. Guest Lecture: First International Outstanding Woman Scholar in Education. Virginia Commonwealth University, Richmond, Virginia, USA, *The Link*: 19–23.

Bruce, T., (1989) Constructive Play. *Child Education*, 66, No. 5: 25–30.

Bruce, T., (1991) *Time to Play in Early Childhood Education*. Sevenoaks: Hodder and Stoughton.

Butler, D., (1987) *Cushla and her Books*. Harmondsworth, Middlesex: Penguin Books Ltd.

Campbell, R.J.; Coates, E.; David, T.; Fitzgerald, J.; Goodyear, R.; Jowett, M.; Lewis, A.; Neil, S.St. J. and Sylva, K., (1990) *Assessing 3–8 year olds*. Windsor: NFER.

Chapman, E.K., (1978) *Visually Handicapped Children and Young People*. London: Routledge and Kegan Paul.

(Ed. comment), (1992) Assess the Scottish way? *Child Education*, 69, No. 8: 4 and 7.

Clay, M., (1985) *The Early Detection of Reading Difficulties*, (3rd edition). London: Heinemann.

Cleave, S. and Brown, S., (1987) *Four-Year-Olds in School: Policy and Practice*. Windsor: NFER/SCDC.

Cleave, S. and Brown, S., (1989) *Four-Year-Olds in School: Meeting Children's Needs*. Windsor: NFER/SCDC.

Cleave, S. and Brown, S., (1991) *Four-Year-Olds in School: Quality Matters*. Windsor: NFER/SCDC.

Cleveland Teachers, (1987) *How Your Child Learns*. Cleveland Department of Education.

Darwin, C., (1877) Biographical sketch of an infant. *Mind.*, 2: 285–294.

David, T. and Lewis, A., (1989) 'Assessment in the reception class' in Harding, L. and Beech, J. (eds). *Assessment in the Primary School*, Windsor: NFER.

David, T., (1900) *Under Five: Under Educated?* Milton Keynes: Open University Press.

Davies, M., (1969) 'Movement: action, feeling and thought' in Brearley, M. (ed.). *Fundamentals in the First School*, Oxford: Blackwell.

Dawes, H.C., (1934) An analysis of two hundred quarrels of pre-school children. *Child Development*, 5: 139–57.

Devon County Council, (1990) *Young Children's Learning: A Curriculum for 3 and 4 Year Olds*. Exeter: Wheaton Publications.

Dewey, J., (1963) *Experience and Education*. New York: First Collier Books (Macmillan Publishing Co).

DES, (1974) *A Language for Life* (The Bullock Report). London: HMSO.

DES, (1988) Task Group on Assessment and Testing: A Report. London: HMSO.

DES, (1989) *Aspects of Primary Education: The Education of Children Under Five*. London: HMSO.

DES, (1989) Report by HM Inspectors on a Survey of Education for 4 Year Olds in Primary Classes. DES Publications Despatch Centre.

DES, (1990) *Starting with Quality:* The Report of Inquiry into the Quality of the Educational Experience offered to 3 and 4 Year Olds. London: HMSO.

DES, (1981) The Implementation of the Curricula Requirements of ERA: an overview of HM Inspectorate on the First Year 1989–1990. London: HMSO.

DES, (1991) The Children Act. Family Support, Day Care and Educational Provision for Young Children: Volume 2. London: HMSO.

DES, (1991) *Working Together Under the Children Act 1989*. A Guide to Arrangements for Inter-agency Co-operation for the Protection of Children from Abuse. London: HMSO.

Donaldson, M., (1978) *Children's Minds*. London: Collins/Fontana.

Drummond, M.J. and Rowse, D., (1992) *Making Assessment Work*. London: National Children's Bureau.

Early Years Curriculum Group, (EYCG) (1989) *Early Childhood Education: The Early Years Curriculum and the National Curriculum*. Stoke-on-Trent: Trentham Books.

Feynman, R., (1981) Horizon Interview: The Pleasure of Finding Things Out. BBC TV.

Froebel, F., (1896) *The Education of Man*. W.N. Hailman trans. New York: Appleton.

Goodman, S., (ed.) (1973) *Miscue Analysis: Application to Reading Instruction*. Urbaba, Illinois: ERIC/NCTE.

Grablucker, M., (W. Philipson trans.) *There's a good girl: gender stereotpying in the first 3 years of life: a diary*. London: Women's Press Ltd, London, 1988.

Gura, P., (ed.) (1992) *Exploring Learning: Young Children and Blockplay*. London: Paul Chapman Publishing Ltd.

Gussin Paley, V., (1985) *Wally's Stories*. London: Heinemann.

Hammersmith and Fulham LEA, (undated) *Nursery Record of Achievement*.

Hammersmith and Fulham LEA, (July, 1991) *Primary Record of Achievement*.

Hardyman, C., (1984) *Dream Babies: Child Care from Locke to Spock*. Oxford: Oxford University Press.

Harlen, W., (1982) Evauation and Assessment, in Richards, C. (ed.). *New Directions in Primary Education*. London: Falmer Press.

Honig, A., (1984) Working in partnership with parents of handicapped infants. *Early Child Development and Care*, 14, Nos. 1–2: 13–36.

Hughes, M.; Wikeley, F. and Nash, P., (July, 1990) *Parents and the National Curriculum. Interim Report*. School of Education, University of Exeter.

Hughes, M.; Wikely, F. and Nash, P., (July, 1991) *Parents and SATS. A Second Interim Report from the Project 'Parents and the National Curriculum'*. School of Education, University of Exeter.

Hurst, V., (1991) *Planning for Early Learning. Education in the First Five Years*. London: Paul Chapman Publishing Ltd.

Irwin, D.M. and Bushnell, M.M., (1980) *Observational Strategies for Child Study*. USA: Holt, Rinehart and Winston.

Isaacs, S., (1930) *Intellectual Growth in Young Children*. New York: Harcourt.

Isaacs, S., (1933) *Social Development in Young Children*. New York: Harcourt.

Isaacs, S., (1968) *The Nursery Years*. London: Routledge and Kegan Paul.

Johnson, H.M., (1933) 'The art of blockbuilding', reprinted in Provenzo, E.F. Jnr. and Brett, A. (1983) *The Complete Block Book*. Syracuse, New York: Syracuse University Press.

Kamii, C., and Devries, R., (1977) (2nd edition). 'Piaget for early years', in Day, M. and Parker R. (eds).*The Pre-school in Action: Exploring Early Childhood Programs*. Newton, Massachusetts: Allyn and Bacon.

Karrby, G., (July, 1989) Children's concepts of their own play, in *The Voice of the Child: Conference Proceedings*. London: OMEP.

Katz, L., (1986) *More Talks with Teachers*. Chapter: Assessing the development of pre-schoolers. Urbana, Illinois: ERIC/EECE.

Lally, M., (1991) *The Nursery Teacher in Action*. London: Paul Chapman Publishing Ltd.

Lothian Regional Council Education Department, (1992) *A Curriculum for the Early Years*.

Matthews, J., (1988) The young child's representation and drawing, in Blenkin, G. and Kelly, V. (eds). *Early Childhood Education. A Developmental Curriculum*. London: Paul Chapman Publishing Ltd.

McCail, G., (1992) *Pre-Five Environment Quality Survey*. Moray House/BAECE.

Merton LEA/R.I.; Devereux, J.; Gifford, S.; Laycock, L.; Stierer, B. and Yerbury, J., (1993). *Profiling, Observing and Recording in the Early Years*. London, Routledge.

Moss, P., (1992) Some implications of the Children Act. *OMEP (UK) Review*, Spring: 17–22.

Moyles, J.R., (1989) *Just Playing? The Role and Status of Play in Early Childhood Education*. Milton Keynes, Philadelphia: Open University Press.

Navarra, J.G., (1955) *The Development of Scientific Concepts in a Young Child. A Case Study*. Bureau of Publications, Teacher College. New York: Columbia University.

Neilsson, L., (1984) Letter in *Information Exchange*. October Issue. Royal National Institute for the Blind.

Neilsson, L., (1985) Letter in *Information Exchange*. September No. 14. Royal National Institute for the Blind.

Nicholls, R. (ed.) with Sedgewick, J.; Duncan, J.; Curwin, L. and McDougall, B., (1986) *Rumpus Schema Extra*. Cleveland Teachers in Education, LEA.

Northamptonshire Schema Working Party, (1990) *Finding Out More About How Children Learn*. Northamptonshire Education Authority.

Northamptonshire LEA, (July, 1992) *First Focus Booklet*.

Nutbrown, C., (1989) Up, down and round. *Child Education*, 66, No. 5: 14–15.

Nutbrown, C., (1989) 'Patterns in paintings, patterns in play. Young Children Learning.' *Topic* 7, Issue 1. Windsor: NFER.

Nutbrown, C., (1991) *Early Literacy Development and Work with Parents. Putting Theory into Practice*. OMEP (UK) Publications Group. Manchester: RMBC.

Ollis, J. with Crachnell, L.; Nicol, E. and Finke, S., (1990) 'Parent held development diaries in practice.' *Early Years*, Volume 10, No. 2: 20–7.

Pascal, C., (1990) *Under-Fives in Infant Classrooms*. Stoke-on-Trent: Trentham Books Ltd.

Pascal, C., (1991–2) Starting with Quality. Four-year-olds in reception classes. *Early Education*, BAECE No. 5, Winter.

Pascal, C., (1992) Advocacy, quality and the education of young children. *Early Years*. TACTYC. Volume 13, No. 1: 5–12.

Pellegrini, A.D., (1991) (2nd edition) *Applied Child Study: A Developmental Approach*. Hillsdale, New Jersey: Lawrence Erlbaum Associates.

Pen Green Centre for Under-Fives and Their Families, (1990) *A Schema Booklet for Parents*. Corby, Northants.

Piaget, J., (1962) *Play, Dreams and Imitation in Childhood*. London: Routledge and Kegan Paul.

Piaget, J. and Inhelder, B., (1969) *The Psychology of the Child*. London: Routledge and Kegan Paul.

Pre-school Playgroups Association, (1991) *What Children Learn in Playgroup. A PPA Guide to the Curriculum*. London: PPA Publication.

Roberts, M. and Tamburrini, J., (eds) (1981) *Child Development 0–5*. Edinburgh: Holmes McDougall.

Robertson, J., (1953) *Film: A Two-Year-Old Goes to Hospital*. 16mm. Snd. 45 minutes. English/French. London: Tavistock Clinic.

Royal National Institute for the Blind, (1993) *Guidelines for Parents of Multi-handicapped Visually Impaired Children*. London: HMSO.

Sestini, E., (1987) The quality of the learning experiences of four-year-olds in nursery and infant classes, in Cleave, S. and Brown, S. (eds) op cit., 26–34.

Sheffield. The City of Sheffield Education Department, (1986) *The Learning and Development of 3–5-Year-Olds. Schema*.

Sheridan, M.D., (1973) *From Birth to Five Years*. Windsor: NFER.

Sheridan, M.D., (1977) *Spontaneous Play in Early Childhood from Birth to 6 Years*. Windsor: NFER/Nelson.

Sylva, K. and Moore, E., (1984) 'A survey of under-fives record-keeping in Great Britain.' *Educational Research*, 26, No. 2: 115–20.

Tamburrini, J., (1981) *Child Development 0–5*, in Roberts, M. and Tamburrini, J. (eds.) op cit.

Tamburrini, J., (1982) 'Some educational implications of Piaget's theory', in Modgil, C. and Modgil, S. (eds). *Piaget: Controversy and Consensus* pp. 309–24. London: Holt, Rinehart and Winston.

Tyler, S., (ed.) (1976) *Pre-school Assessment Guide*. Windsor: NFER/Nelson.

Webb, L., (1975) *Making a Start on Child Study*. Oxford: Basil Blackwell.

Weinberger, J.; Hannon, P. and Nutbrown, C., (1990) *Ways of Working with Parents to Promote Literacy Development*. Department of Education, University of Sheffield.

Weir, R., (1962) *Language in the Crib*. The Hague: Mouton.

Wells, G., (1983) 'Talking with children: the complementary roles of parents and teachers', in Donaldson, M.; Grieve, R. and Pratt, C. (eds). *Early Childhood Development and Education*. Oxford: Basil Blackwell.

Wells, G., (1987) *The Meaning Makers*. Sevenoaks: Hodder and Stoughton.

West, P., (1972) *Words for a Deaf Daughter*. Harmondsworth, Middlesex: Penguin Books Ltd.

Whalley, M., (1993) *Learning to be Strong: Setting up a Neighbourhood Service for Under-Fives and Their Families*. Sevenoaks: Hodder and Stoughton.

Whitehead, M., (1992) Core subjects and the developmental curriculum, in Blenkin, G. and Kelly, V. (eds). *Assessment in Early Childhood Education*. London: Paul Chapman Publishing Ltd.

Wolfendale, S., (1987) *All About Me*. Psychology Department, N.E. London Polytechnic.

Index